RE-IMAGINE YOU

BioRegenesis of the DNA Blueprint through Source Feeding

DR. CAROL TALBOT

GULF BOOK SERVICES

Published by Gulf Book Services Ltd
20-22 Wenlock Road, London,
NI 7GU, UK
Email: info@gulfbooks.co.uk
Office No: G23,
Sharjah Publishing City Freezone
Sharjah – UAE

GULF BOOK SERVICES

First Published by Gulf Book Services Ltd

ISBN: 978-1-917529-07-5
Year: December 2024

This book is dedicated to:

The pursuit of possibilities—may you always seek out the unknown, daring to imagine what lies beyond the horizon of your current understanding. Challenging what you have been taught and told— may you question the status quo with courage, allowing yourself the freedom to unlearn and relearn, breaking free from the confines of inherited beliefs. Exploring new paradigms—may you venture into the realms of the unconventional, embracing the wisdom of alternative perspectives and pioneering the pathways to a new way of being. Becoming more than you ever thought you could be—may you recognize the boundless potential within you, unlocking layers of your true essence, and stepping into a life of greater purpose, power, and possibility.

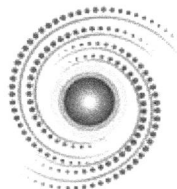

Contents

Foreword

Dr. Carol's brilliant work in the bioregenesis of our DNA and the expansion of higher levels of conscious identity offers profound support for those who are ready to unlock their full, eternal human potential. By bridging the cutting-edge science of eternal life with ancient pre-historical knowledge, she facilitates transformative shifts in humanity's understanding of its own re-evolution.

Dr. Carol exemplifies what becomes possible when we reconnect with the Source Consciousness field, allowing our original, limitless potential to unfold and flourish naturally.

Dr. Jere Rivera-Dugenio, Ph.D.

Pioneer in Quantum Morphogenetic Physics, Creator of the revolutionary RASHA® technology

Re-Imagine
YOU

Introduction

I held my hand up in front of me... it had vanished. I brought it closer to my face, but still, there was nothing. Were my eyes open or closed? I couldn't tell. All I knew was that I was cocooned in profound darkness—one that felt like it reached beyond the mere absence of light and into a space where deeper truths slumbered, waiting to stir. This was the beginning of my darkroom experience - a place where sight became irrelevant, and the mysteries of the unseen world began to unfold.

But this journey didn't truly begin in that pitch-black room. It started long before, with a spark of curiosity that ignited my quest for knowledge—knowledge hidden in the corners of reality, where few dare to look. I've always been drawn to teachings that challenge the limits of what we think we know, seeking out those elusive truths that hover just beyond perception. I searched for answers through countless books, programs, and retreats, and not all roads led to clarity; some were tangled in illusions and deceptions.

Many years ago, while visiting my mother, I stumbled upon an old manual she had tucked away, untouched for twenty-five years. It was filled with strange symbols and cryptic instructions, and though she struggled with its meaning, I, too, set it aside, unsure of its relevance. Little did I know that this forgotten manual held the key to a path I wasn't yet ready to walk.

Then, a year later, I encountered a lecture that reignited the embers of my curiosity, unlocking forgotten insights about our origins and the descent from Source consciousness into physical form. I felt an undeniable pull, a recognition that I had stumbled upon something crucial. This was the gateway to a body of knowledge that stretched my understanding of reality beyond anything I had imagined.

The truth can disguise itself in the most unexpected places, only revealing itself when we are truly ready to see. What I found took me on a journey through the mysteries of true DNA activation, the physics of multidimensionality, and the hidden potential within us all. Each discovery peeled back another layer of reality, leading me here—to the very reason I wrote this book: *Re-Imagine YOU*

This is more than just a book. It's an invitation to awaken to the wisdom embedded within you, to remember your limitless potential. As you turn these pages, may you feel a resonance—not of something new—but of a deep truth you have always known. Let this be the spark that guides you back to the brilliance of who you truly are.

PREVIEW

PART ONE - UNVEILING THE POTENTIAL

Imagine your DNA as the key to unlocking the extraordinary potential within you—a potential suppressed by societal conditioning and mass programming. This section reveals how understanding your genetic makeup holds the secret to transcending limitations and reclaiming your true multidimensional self. Discover the profound connection between DNA, consciousness, and Higher Sensory Perception and how Masters and Gurus may have activated their DNA to achieve what seems impossible. To unleash our own potential, we must first disconnect from the mass programming and conditioning that has hindered our progress.

PART TWO - UNVEILING THE BLUEPRINT

The human DNA blueprint has been dormant for thousands of years, limiting your natural ability to embody higher consciousness and activate Higher Sensory Perception. But it's time to remember. This section calls you to awaken to your original agenda as a human. By reigniting the dormant codes within your DNA, you'll begin to merge with your true spiritual identity, unlocking memories long lost and reconnecting with the earth, higher dimensions, and the grand design of your creation. Bioregenesis is the path to healing, longevity, and unlocking your full evolutionary potential.

PART THREE - CONTAMINATED

Now begins the exploration of a radical concept - Source Feeding. What if nourishment went far beyond physical food? In a world where food and water are often tainted, Source Feeding offers an alternative—a way to heal, thrive, and sustain yourself through pure pranic energy. This section takes you to the heart of a controversial yet compelling idea:

by harnessing the life force energy surrounding us, we can transcend physical sustenance, restore vitality, and reclaim our limitless potential. Bioregenesis begins here, in the shift from dependency on material food to nourishment from energy.

PART FOUR - REIMAGINING NOURISHMENT

Prepare to expand your perception of what it means to be nourished. In this section, you'll dive deeper into the energetic dimensions of sustenance. Imagine drawing life-giving energy from nature, colors, sounds, and even your own thoughts. As you open yourself to this energetic world, you'll find a limitless well of vitality and fulfillment. By reimagining your relationship with the energy that flows all around and within you, the door opens to a life of greater purpose, sustained not by food alone but by the vibrant forces of the universe.

PART FIVE - EMBARKING ON THE PATH OF SOURCE FEEDING

In this final section, you'll accompany me on some of my most profound and life-changing experiences. Together, we will explore Source Feeding through my personal accounts of Dark Room Technology and dry fasting—practices that reveal a reality far beyond what conventional wisdom suggests. These experiences have reshaped my understanding of nourishment, vitality, and what it truly means to thrive. Join me as we peel back the layers of what is possible for human potential and, perhaps, for your own transformation

PART ONE

Unveiling the Potential:

Exploring Superhuman Abilities, Higher Sensory
Perception, and Navigating the Maze

"You are always more than you think you are."

I stood there, my breath caught in my throat as the bright orange coals, glowing with intensity, shimmered in the dark just inches from my bare feet. All day, I'd waited for someone to say, "It's cool as moss," or guide us into a trance, chanting, "It's cool as ice." But that moment never came. Instead, they simply reminded us of one thing: those coals were *hot.*

We had built the fire hours earlier, and as the sun sank behind the horizon, the fire dwindled, leaving behind the burning remnants of 1,700 degrees Fahrenheit of blistering heat, ready for us to cross. I watched others stride over the coals one by one, and soon it was my turn. I stood there, staring down at the fiery path. In that instant, a voice in my head screamed, "Are you nuts, Carol?" An image of my feet, black and charred, flashed before me.

Yet, despite the panic in my mind, something deeper, an inner knowing, told me it was possible. I could feel it in my heart. But my mind, ever the guardian of caution, rebelled, warning me of the dangers. I hesitated as the heat washed over me. I took a deep breath... and stepped back away from the coals.

My fascination with superhuman abilities has taken me far and wide, from exploring ancient practices to teaching breakthrough experiences like firewalking. People often ask me, "Why?" Why pursue these extreme challenges?

It's never been about the spectacle or the thrill alone. Something far deeper is at work here and a powerful, transformative energy that stirs within. As a Master Fire-walk Instructor, I've guided individuals and organizations through this remarkable journey for over 20 years. And still, I marvel at how firewalking can unlock hidden potential in hours, revealing depths of strength people never knew they had.

Firewalking is one of humanity's oldest rituals for transformation. Across the globe, cultures have walked across hot coals, not for show, but as a sacred act honoring the fire as a force of healing, purification, and personal evolution. In Bali, the children walk the coals, unburdened by fear, dancing across the embers as if they were born to do it. In ancient temples, priests and priestesses used firewalking as a path to healing. From tribes to civilizations, firewalking has been a universal tool to empower, heal, and ignite change, nourishing the human spirit for millennia. Yet, today, its profound benefits are largely forgotten or misunderstood.

That first time standing before the fiery path, I felt the conflict within— fear versus the undeniable desire to rise above my limitations. I was determined to move beyond the boundaries of my mind. Gathering every ounce of courage, I quieted the inner voice, focused my mind, and stepped forward. With each step across the glowing coals, I felt an electric connection to something greater, a force untouchable by doubt or fear. When I reached the other side, I rushed to wash my feet, bracing myself for the evidence of my ordeal. To my astonishment, there wasn't a single mark on them.

At that moment, I felt invincible, like I had tapped into a reservoir of untapped potential. It was clear: I had accessed a power within me, waiting to be awakened.

From a scientific standpoint, fire-walking and the extraordinary phenomena that come with it are often dismissed, challenging the conventional limits of human sensory perception. But what if these experiences invite you to question the boundaries you think exist? What if they're a gateway to the extraordinary abilities everyone possesses? The possibilities are limitless if you surpass your fears and embrace the unknown.

Chapter One:

Masters & Superhumans
and the Potential of Higher Sensory Perception

KEY QUESTIONS:

What are you really capable of?

What is your true potential?

In 1924, Life and Teachings of the Masters of the Far East by Baird T. Spalding captured the world's imagination, recounting the remarkable journey of eleven scientists who traveled to India and Tibet in search of the great spiritual teachers of the Himalayas. What they found was beyond anything they could have anticipated - immortal beings, known as the Great Masters, whose existence defied conventional understanding of human capability.

These masters didn't just teach spiritual wisdom; they embodied it in impossible ways. The scientists claimed to have witnessed firsthand their extraordinary abilities—walking on water, appearing in two places at once, and even manifesting food out of thin air to feed the hungry party. At the same time, the masters themselves lived without food or water, sustained entirely by prana, the life force that permeates the universe. These weren't miracles reserved for divine beings. According to the Masters, these abilities lie dormant within all of us.

Imagine for a moment: what if you could tap into this same power? What if the boundaries of what you thought possible were merely illusions waiting to be shattered?

Spalding's books reveal that these so-called miracles are not in the realm of the impossible but instead a natural expression of human potential. Master Puriji, one of the Masters described in the books, explained that abilities like levitation and what many would call supernatural are simply the result of knowing and mastering one's true self. He said Buddha could use this very power to travel to distant lands, and even more astonishing feats, like moving mountains, are possible for those who unlock the full force of this innate energy.

The question is, what else might you be capable of? What hidden potential lies within you, waiting to be discovered? As you begin this journey, allow yourself to wonder not just about these ancient abilities but about the untapped power you may hold and what might happen when you choose to awaken it.

Superhuman Feats Throughout History

The idea of becoming superhuman has fascinated mankind for eons. Emperors of bygone eras searched for the elixirs of immortality, Shaolin monks have pushed the limits of what is possible with the body for thousands of years, and the old alchemists searched for ways to transmute metals into gold.

There are the Kahunas & Polynesian Shamans, often called the Masters of Reality. Before Christian missionaries and encroaching Western culture effectively stamped out Polynesian spiritual traditions in the later part of the 20th century, Hawaii was a hotbed of Kahuna activity, with powerful shamans regularly and openly demonstrating a long list of extraordinary superpowers.

There are literally hundreds of documented case studies and firsthand accounts of extraordinary superhuman feats being performed by the Kahunas, ranging from walking on scorching hot lava for extended periods of time and instantly healing life-threatening wounds, broken bones, and any disease in a matter of seconds, to the instant materialization of physical objects, levitation, the ability to manipulate reality in their favor, the ability to contact and interact with spirits at will, the ability to teleport and bilocate, the ability to see into the future and past at will and to project their consciousness nearly anywhere on the planet or in the universe and observe what they saw.

Decoding Esoteric Knowledge

Much of this became known due to a budding scientist and parapsychological researcher named Max Freedom Long, who found himself on the Hawaiian Islands in the early part of the 19th century. Fascinated with superhuman abilities, he quickly became intrigued by the stories he heard about the Kahunas from the Hawaiians, who had gained his trust. Through synchronistic events, he finally got in contact with real Kahunas, who could actively demonstrate the supernatural powers outlined above. However, they categorically refused to reveal any of their secrets as it was forbidden to do so to non-Polynesians in their cultural traditions.

Eventually, Long found a way to access the miraculous secrets he sought by decoding the Hawaiian language. By studying Hawaiian and Polynesian languages and through a multi-year-long practice of trial and error, Long eventually unlocked their secrets and began to gain access to their legendary powers.

Fascinatingly, the esoteric knowledge he found hidden in their language, which had been passed down as spiritual wisdom for thousands of years, was not only up to speed with what Western psychologists in Europe and the U.S. had discovered about the nature and structure of the mind, but it was far more nuanced and sophisticated. More recently, scientific studies have increasingly highlighted the profound influence of language and thoughts on DNA expression and cellular function.

Modern Miracles

Imagine witnessing a man who could materialize objects out of thin air with a mere wave of his hand. In India, Sathya Sai Baba was revered as one of the most extraordinary avatars of modern times, a spiritual teacher whose supernatural feats baffled the minds of millions. From bilocating—being in two places at once—to instant healing and even resurrecting the dead, Sai Baba's abilities seemed to transcend the very laws of nature. Perhaps the most famous of his powers was his ability to manifest physical objects effortlessly using nothing but the sheer force of his consciousness. Sacred ash, jewels, and holy relics appeared in his hands as if summoned from the very fabric of the universe.

Countless firsthand accounts and videos witness these phenomena, with entire rooms filled with devotees watching in awe as Sai Baba performed what appeared to be miracles. Skeptics may dismiss him as a master illusionist, but those who experienced his teachings knew something far more significant. His profound message, rooted in all humans' divine nature, inspired millions to question the limits of their reality.

Such abilities, often relegated to myth or magic, are not unique to Sai Baba. In the ancient Hindu text, Patanjali's Yoga Sutras, 19 supernatural powers, or siddhis, are outlined and attainable through deep yogic practice. Among them are feats such as the ability to disappear from view, levitate, control the elements, and transcend the need for food and water. Imagine living without hunger or thirst, defying the conventional medical understanding of the human body. These siddhis reveal a truth that defies logic, powers that place the practitioner on the brink of what most would call impossible.

Mastering all 19 siddhis is legendary and a mark of profound understanding that unites mind, body, and spirit in ways beyond our current comprehension. As the ancient texts tell us, these powers are not miracles reserved for the chosen few; they are human abilities that are latent in you and waiting to be awakened.

Beyond the Five Senses

What if these powers, these siddhis, are just the beginning? What if I told you that your five senses are only the tip of the iceberg? Ashayana Deane, a visionary teacher, proposes a radical and awe-inspiring idea: that you have not five but twelve senses, each a gateway to perceiving higher dimensions of reality. What we call extrasensory perception (ESP), abilities like clairvoyance and telepathy are not rare gifts for the few but a natural attribute of your evolving human potential.

Consider your senses as translators, decoding the energy around you into experiences. When you smell a flower, your nose is not simply detecting a fragrance; it's translating energy into a sensory experience. Now imagine the potential of more senses, each capable of perceiving realities and energies far beyond what your current senses allow.

According to Deane, these dormant senses are linked to your DNA, which acts as a bridge between your body and higher-dimensional energies. The blockages within your DNA, caused by distortions, prevent you from fully accessing these heightened perceptions. It's like having a weak Wi-Fi signal that limits your connection to the vast, multidimensional web of reality. By repairing your DNA, you can enhance your neurogenesis, thereby creating new neurons in the brain, which improve memory, learning, and intuition and unlock the potential for clairvoyance and other psychic abilities.

But here's the incredible part: individuals who display ESP aren't supernatural; they're simply further along in their natural evolution. They've cleared the blockages that hold most people back and tapped into the full power of their senses. They represent the next stage of human development, and this potential also exists within you.

Think of it this way: your senses, when fully activated, can access the deeper, richer layers of reality that remain hidden from view. Clairvoyance, clairaudience, and clairsentience are not "gifts" bestowed on a lucky few; they are abilities and skills that can be honed and developed. With the right practices and the healing of your DNA, you can unlock these dormant senses and experience the world in ways you never imagined.

Deane's work suggests that beyond the traditional senses of sight, sound, touch, smell, and taste (rooted in the lower dimensions), seven more senses correspond to higher dimensions of reality. These senses are linked to the activation of currently dormant DNA strands. When fully awakened, they will allow you to perceive and interact with the higher-dimensional aspects of existence.

Are you ready to discover what the Higher Dimensional Senses can open up for you?

Higher Dimensional Sense Faculties & Primary Attribute

Manifestation (Circulation of Consciousness and Frequency Accretion):

This refers to how our thoughts and energy shape our reality. By focusing our consciousness, we gather or "accrete" energy (frequency), which helps bring things into existence or change our environment.

Imagine visualizing something you deeply desire, like a new job. As you consistently focus on it, you gather energy (positive thoughts, emotions, and actions) that align with that goal, helping it manifest in your life.

Cellular Telepathy (Inner Audio-Visual Direct Cognition Reading Energy Signatures)

This is like an intuitive way of "reading" others or the environment by focusing on their energy. It's not through words but through direct perception of energy patterns. For example, you meet someone and instantly feel like you know what they're about—

without them saying a word. You might "see" images or "hear" a sense of what's happening in their life just from being near them.

Transmutation Sense (Molecular Transmutation and Shape Shifting):

This refers to the ability to change the structure of matter, including your form. It's about shifting from one state to another. In mythology, some beings are said to shape-shift into animals. On a subtler level, this could also mean being able to shift how you're perceived or even changing your emotional energy from fear to love.

Transmigration Sense (Projection of Consciousness):

This is the ability to project your awareness outside of your physical body and experience different locations or realities, for example, through astral projection, where people report leaving their body and traveling to distant places in their mind or spirit, which is a form of this sense.

Transfiguration Sense (Bi-location and Multiple Holographic Manifestations):

This refers to being able to exist in more than one place simultaneously or showing up in different forms in different spaces.

Some spiritual teachers are said to appear to people in multiple locations at once, such as the Masters cited in Spalding's books. In quantum physics, it's like particles existing in different places simultaneously.

Centrifugal Sense (Electrical Projection and Entering Dimensionalization):

This involves sending energy outward, helping consciousness enter new layers of reality or dimensions.

Imagine sending out your energy to explore higher realms of existence, like sensing or interacting with beings or energies in another dimension.

    Centripetal Sense (Magnetic Accretion and Exiting Dimensionalization):

This is the opposite of centrifugal—pulling energy inward, allowing consciousness to exit from dimensions and return to a pure state of being. For example, after exploring different realms of consciousness, you return to a state of stillness or pure awareness, like meditation, where you feel deeply connected to a universal oneness.

These concepts describe advanced abilities and states of consciousness beyond typical human experience, often associated with higher dimensions of existence. They can be likened to the 'superpowers' described in Patanjali's Yoga Sutras, the Hawaiian Kahunas, Polynesian Shamans, Sai Baba, and the Masters and Gurus of the Far East. These traditions remind us that such abilities are not the stuff of legend but intrinsic to the fabric of human potential, waiting to be rediscovered.

Neurogenesis and DNA Repair

Consider the genetic code a grand, intricate symphony written for an orchestra. Over time, however, certain music sections have been covered with dust, and some instruments have fallen silent. The human perceptual field, with its blockages, acts like layers of dust and cobwebs, muffling the sound and obscuring the notes. But what if we could sweep away these blockages and restore the full expression of our symphony - reawakening dormant abilities and even repairing our DNA?

As you begin to clear away these blockages, it is like a diligent conductor and a team of restorers meticulously removing the dust from a musical score, uncovering the hidden notes, and bringing the silent instruments back into play. With each note restored and each instrument reawakened, the symphony becomes richer and more complex, revealing nuances and harmonies previously unheard.

This reawakening of the symphony corresponds to the genetic code reassembling and activating dormant segments of the DNA. The restored music transforms the orchestra's performance as these segments come to life. The tempo (metabolic rate) quickens, the musicians' coordination (brain activity) improves, the flow of the music (blood circulation) becomes more dynamic, the resonance (glandular and hormonal function) deepens, the precision sharpens, and the overall harmony (Central Nervous System operation) becomes more profound.

These enhancements in the symphony's performance allow the audience (the human perceptual field) to experience the music in a new way, perceiving layers and dimensions of sound (higher sense faculties) that were previously inaudible. The once-muted symphony now expands into a full, multi-dimensional realm of sound, illustrating how the activation of the genetic code facilitates an expanded and enriched human experience. Your body becomes more attuned to the energy of life, and you start to perceive reality in ways you never thought possible.

Unlocking Your Higher Senses

This awakening is more than just a physical shift - it's a shift in perception. As these dormant parts of your DNA come online, your senses expand. You start to notice things you couldn't before, like subtle energy shifts or thoughts that seem to manifest quickly in your reality. Have you ever thought of someone just before they called or texted you? That's a small example of what happens when your higher senses begin to wake up.

As this process unfolds, something extraordinary happens. Your mind and body work together in ways beyond the five senses you've always known. You might begin to experience telepathy—hearing or sensing things from others without speaking—or even see visions or receive intuitive information from a deeper, more connected part of yourself. These aren't magic tricks; they're abilities that have been lying dormant within you, waiting for the right conditions to awaken.

For most people, these higher senses remain out of reach. Why? Because our DNA, much like a radio tuned to only one station, is 'phase-locked' into a narrow, three-dimensional reality. It's like tuning into a higher frequency, but static gets in the way. The static, or distortions, in your DNA is what mainstream science calls "junk DNA." These distortions block the natural flow of higher-dimensional energy, keeping most people from experiencing their full potential.

And yet, the possibilities are immense. When these blockages are cleared and your DNA is repaired, you begin to tap into the higher dimensions of reality, where your senses expand and your consciousness evolves. You start to notice that what once seemed like dreams or intuition becomes sharper, more real, and more frequent. This isn't some far-off fantasy; it's the next step in human evolution and within your reach.

Unfortunately, many people remain unaware of these latent abilities, held back by mass programming and the limitations placed on our collective consciousness. But the truth is that you have the power to unlock these higher senses, to step into a reality where your thoughts, intentions, and perceptions can transform your life experience.

The question is: are you ready to clear the static and awaken the full symphony of your DNA?

Re-Imagine
YOU

Superhuman abilities are not just relics of the past. Today, some individuals continue to demonstrate extraordinary feats that challenge our understanding of human potential. Wim Hof, known as the Iceman, uses an ancient meditation technique to maintain his body temperature in extreme cold. His practice, rooted in Tummo meditation, showcases the power of the mind over the body.

John Chang, the Magus of Java, is a Chinese Neigong practitioner who has developed an extraordinary level of control over the body's subtle energies. His abilities, including lighting fires with his hands and healing the sick, highlight the incredible potential of focused energy cultivation.

Master Zhou, a Qi Gong Grand Master, demonstrates similar abilities, such as raising water temperature with his hands and setting paper on fire using only his energy. These feats illustrate the power of harnessing and focusing internal energy to achieve extraordinary results.

My own experiences have shown me that superhuman abilities are not just theoretical but achievable with dedication, focus, and belief.

Just for a moment, consider the human body's extraordinary capacity for healing and regeneration, guided by its innate intelligence. This remarkable self-healing ability is orchestrated through a complex interplay of cellular processes, genetic programming, and environmental responses.

For example, in terms of cellular renewal:

- **Skin:** Renews every 28 days, with the outer layer regenerating every 2 to 4 weeks.
- **Liver:** Can regrow up to 70% of its tissue within weeks after injury.

Bones: The entire skeleton is renewed approximately every 10 years.

Now reflect on your current reality and realize:

⟹ **You are a creator**:
Your external world reflects your inner thoughts.
Are you creating an environment of harmony or dissonance?

⟹ **You are a healer**:
Your body has an innate ability to heal. Have you noticed how quickly a bruise or scratch disappears?

⟹ **You are limitless**:
Have you ever accomplished something you once thought impossible? You have the power to turn the impossible into the possible.

The exploration of superhuman abilities invites you to reconsider the limits of human potential and the true essence of your individual journey of self-discovery and expansion. By cultivating a superhuman mindset, you can tap into your innate capacities and open the door to new possibilities.

"You are more powerful than you realize. The journey to becoming superhuman begins with the belief that you already are."

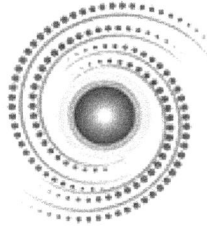

Chapter Two

Navigating the Maze:
Understanding Mass Programming
& Conditioning

KEY QUESTIONS:

What if everything you've been taught and told is wrong?
How do you discover your own truth?

Do you wake up with an alarm clock every day? Do you leap out of bed, eager to greet the day, or do you hit the snooze button, craving just a few more minutes of rest?

You stop when you're driving and see a red traffic light, right?

And what about when you're at work, and a meeting is called? Do you think, 'Fantastic, an opportunity to share my creative ideas,' or is it more like, 'Oh no, another meeting?'

Or maybe someone looks at you in a certain way, and your heart melts—or perhaps you feel a sudden sense of dread.

These are all examples of conditioned responses. The alarm clock is a trigger. What's your reaction? The red light is a signal, and you've been conditioned to respond with a stop for red and go for green, haven't you?

What if these automatic responses run deeper? Have you ever considered how many of your actions are dictated by conditioning rather than conscious choice? Are you simply a finely tuned machine responding to external cues without even thinking about it?

This brings us to the fascinating field of cybernetics, which explores communication and control in both living organisms and machines. It raises thought-provoking questions about human behavior. One theory suggests that we might operate like sophisticated robots—meticulously conditioned to respond in specific, predictable ways. This challenges the idea of free will, implying that much of what you do is dictated by an intricate web of stimuli and responses, like a machine following instructions.

Now, think back to your school days. Have you ever questioned whether what you learned was truly useful in your life? I often wonder why we weren't taught essential life skills, such as critical thinking, conflict resolution, or how the mind really works. Why were we not encouraged to develop natural psychic abilities or explore the human body's miraculous healing power? Instead, we were fed information, often without questioning its relevance—or even its truth.

It makes you wonder how many of your conditioned responses were intentionally created. Who set those triggers, and for what purpose? Could it be that you've been systematically steered away from realizing your true potential and extraordinary abilities, talents, and gifts through education and society? What if the world around you and everything you've learned was designed not to elevate you but to condition you? And if that's the case, how do you break free?

The journey to uncover the truth begins with recognizing the triggers and responses that dictate your daily life and questioning the systems that created them. The more you wake up to this reality, the more you can begin to reclaim your autonomy.

The Origins of Conditioned Behavior

The concept of conditioned response has a long and fascinating history. While many credit the Russian psychologist Ivan Pavlov for its discovery, the roots actually trace back to an earlier study. In 1902, Dr. Edwin B. Twitmyer presented a paper called "Stimulus Response" to the American Medical Association. Unfortunately, the importance of this work was overlooked at the time, but Pavlov recognized its potential and began his own experiments—this time with dogs.

Pavlov's breakthrough came when he repeatedly placed steak in front of the dogs, causing them to salivate. Each time they salivated, he would ring a bell. After many repetitions, something remarkable happened: Pavlov found that just ringing the bell alone would make the dogs salivate, even in the absence of food. The neutral sound bell had become a powerful trigger, creating an automatic response. In 1936, after years of this work, Pavlov submitted his findings to the Russian Medical Society under the name "Conditioned Reflexes," forever changing our understanding of behavior.

Now, what does this mean for you? As a human being, you are not so different from Pavlov's dogs in this respect—you too are a conditioned response machine. For instance, when your stomach growls, you've been conditioned to associate that signal with hunger and the need to eat. But it's not just hunger; any of your five senses can trigger a conditioned response.

Take smell, for example. The scent of freshly cut grass might instantly transport you to childhood memories of your father mowing the lawn, while for someone else, the aroma of freshly brewed coffee sparks a wave of comfort and pleasure. Hearing a particular song can reignite memories of a great vacation or an unforgettable night out. These responses, woven into your senses, have been conditioned over time, creating powerful triggers that guide your behavior—often without you even realizing it.

However, it's not all positive. Just as you've formed happy associations, you've also developed negative responses. Perhaps someone's expression causes you to feel nervous or threatened, or your partner leaving the toothpaste cap off sparks irritation, no matter how trivial the act. These automatic responses shape your daily habits, building a powerful network of reactions that influence your actions.

Many research studies suggest that up to 95% of what we do daily is driven by habit, particularly when we factor in unconscious routines like moving, eating, or thinking. These ingrained behaviors often occur without us even being aware of them, making them an even more powerful force in shaping our lives. By recognizing how much of our daily activity is on autopilot, we can see the immense potential for change when we consciously rewire those habits. While habits can help you excel in certain areas, they can also trap you in unproductive or unhealthy behavior cycles. Maybe you reach for a cookie when stressed or crave something sugary when anxious. Perhaps this habit was formed when, as a child, you were given candy to soothe your worries. Over time, these conditioned responses take root, dictating your actions and how you cope with life's challenges.

What if you could break free from these automatic responses and rewrite your conditioning? Understanding how these patterns are formed is the first step toward reclaiming control so you can consciously choose new, empowering habits that align with the life you truly want to live. The key lies in recognizing your triggers and then reshaping your responses. The question is—how will you begin to recondition your life?

The Subtle Art of Conditioning Through Society

Mass programming, in various forms such as societal conditioning, cultural norms, and media influence, has played a significant role in creating conditioned responses, obscuring knowledge about Higher Senses, and inhibiting their development. Through subtle messaging, societal constructs, and reinforcement of materialistic values, you are subtly coerced into conforming to a limited paradigm that neglects the deeper aspects of human perception and potential.

The relentless bombardment of distractions, superficial entertainment, and consumerism further reinforces this ignorance and complacency, diverting attention away from introspection and spiritual exploration. As la result, the vast majority of people remain unaware of the untapped capabilities within themselves and the broader scope of existence beyond the material realm.

Consider for a moment that from the moment you are born, you are given a name, placed into a religion, sent to school and taught a history that may or may not be true. You are then tested on what you have been told and taught, and if you accept what is told and taught, you get high marks at school, rewards, and accolades, and you are told you are a good student. You are also taught and told what is possible and what is not. If you have been taught and told that if, for example, you put your hand in the fire, you will burn your hand, that it's impossible to walk across water or live without physical food and nourish the physical body in an alternative way, then that is what you come to believe and therefore are basically programmed, conditioned and placed into a limited paradigm.

The Hidden Architects of Mass Control

This belief paradigm is not accidental but, in many cases, the result of deliberate social engineering. One prominent institution involved in such efforts is the Tavistock Institute in London, founded in 1921 and often referred to as the Freud Hilton, as Sigmund Freud's daughter, Dr Anna Freud, became a leading figure there. It was later taken over by Dr John Rawlings Rees, a key figure in British Army Intelligence and previously a top psychiatric warfare specialist. Upgraded in 1947 to the outside world, it was known as a social science research organization. Yet underneath this facade, its main purpose has been mass programming and manipulating human behavior.

Tavistock engages in social engineering projects to shape public opinion, control societal norms, and influence political outcomes. The institute's work in the field of social science and psychology is often cited as evidence of its alleged influence over public behavior. Of course, there are other such organizations.

A huge amount of funding has been allocated to some of these other foundations aligned with the Tavistock Institute in terms of the mental and psychological life of people on the planet, all stored in computer systems.

What is the purpose of this monitoring, profiling, and behavior modification? Is it all to support you in living a healthier, wealthier, and happier life and actualizing your true potential? Sadly, these manipulations will change your way of life, tear apart your inner sense of identity, and shift you further away from your sovereignty and true human abilities.

How Propaganda Shapes Perception

The concept of mass programming through subliminal messaging has long intrigued and alarmed many, particularly in the realms of media manipulation and societal control. At the heart of this issue lies the undeniable influence of television—a powerful tool scrutinized for its role in shaping public opinion and behavior.

Enter Edward Bernays, the so-called father of modern propaganda. Nephew of Sigmund Freud, Bernays revolutionized the art of persuasion by applying his uncle's psychological principles to the masses. His ability to manipulate public perception was nothing short of groundbreaking, and his strategic efforts introduced Freud's psychoanalysis to America.

Bernays believed the masses were malleable and easily influenced by carefully curated information. His early 20th-century work laid the foundation for today's sophisticated media and political tactics. One of his most famous campaigns, the 1929 "Torches of Freedom" event, perfectly exemplified his mastery. Tasked with making cigarettes socially acceptable for women, Bernays orchestrated a parade where debutantes publicly smoked Lucky Strike cigarettes, framing it as an act of female empowerment. By cleverly linking smoking to freedom, he shattered the taboo and expanded the market for women smokers.

But Bernays' influence didn't stop with consumerism. His tactics extended to political manipulation, such as his involvement in the 1954 Guatemalan coup. His work paved the way for mass control through media, particularly television. With its unparalleled reach, TV has become a vehicle for shaping societal norms, subtly crafting perceptions with every broadcast. After all, they're called "television programs" for a reason—each time we tune in, we're being programmed, whether we realize it or not.

The Hidden Influence on Your Consciousness

With its ever-presence in modern life, television serves as a conduit for disseminating information, entertainment, and cultural narratives. Beneath its surface lurks the subtle influence of subliminal messaging, a technique aimed at bypassing the conscious mind to implant ideas, suggestions, and subliminal messages directly into the unconscious mind.

One of the most powerful movies about subliminal messages and mass programming that you may have come across is called "They Live," a 1988 film that follows a drifter who travels to Los Angeles for a job. While on the street, he comes across a street preacher warning that the rich and powerful have been recruited to control humanity.

That night, a hacker takes over television broadcasts, claiming that scientists have discovered signals enslaving the population and keeping them in a dream-like state and that the only way to stop it is to shut off the signal at its source. Those watching the broadcast complain of headaches. The following day, the drifter retrieves a box from where the broadcast took place and takes a pair of sunglasses. He discovers that the sunglasses make the world appear monochrome, in other words, in black and white, but they also reveal subliminal messages in the media to consume, obey, reproduce, and conform. The glasses also reveal that many people are aliens with skull-like faces.

Just as the sunglasses reveal hidden truths in the world around us, hypnosis unveils the deeper layers of the mind, where perceptions can be altered and reality reshaped.

Hypnosis and the Unconscious Mind

In hypnosis, you enter a relaxed state of focused attention, often guided by a hypnotherapist. During this state, the conscious mind becomes partially suspended, allowing suggestions to be more readily accepted by the unconscious mind. In this state, you may be more open to suggestions or imagery that influence your thoughts, perceptions, and behaviors.

Both subliminal messages and hypnosis aim to access and influence the unconscious mind, and they differ in their approach and depth of influence. Subliminal messages attempt to bypass conscious awareness altogether, while hypnosis involves a state of heightened suggestibility within the conscious mind. Both can potentially impact behavior negatively or positively.

While both subliminal messages and hypnosis target the unconscious mind, their influence can extend beyond mere suggestions. The impact becomes even more pronounced when we consider the role of modern media, particularly television. When watching TV, the brain's activity shifts predominantly to the right hemisphere, triggering a release of natural opiates like endorphins and enkephalins. These chemicals, strikingly similar to opium and its derivatives, can create a powerful, almost addictive response, further amplifying the mind's susceptibility to external influences.

How Mass Programming Impacts Your Health

Television works as a very efficient drug delivery system.
Another effect of watching television is that the higher brain regions, such as the mid-brain and the neo-cortex, are shut down, and most activity shifts to the limbic system, which is the lower brain region. The lower or reptilian brain stands poised to react to the environment using deeply embedded fight or flight response programs. Moreover, these lower brain regions cannot distinguish reality from fabricated images, so they react to television content as though it were real, releasing appropriate hormones. Studies have now proved that over time, too

much activity in the lower brain leads to atrophy in the higher brain regions.

How does this relate to your limited view of reality and your abilities?

Television and now the internet, through advertisements, news broadcasts, and entertainment programs, began subtly incorporating elements designed to influence attitudes and beliefs. The blurred line between content and advertising, often unnoticed by viewers, underscores the effectiveness of subliminal messaging in shaping collective consciousness and ensuring we are firmly limited to the lower five senses and that Higher Sensory Perception lies in the realms of fantasy and fiction.

As this subtle manipulation of consciousness through television and the internet took hold, it extended beyond visual content to the realm of sound. Philosopher of Modern Music and Frankfurt School leader Theodor Adorno argued that modern music itself is designed with a purpose—to destabilize the listener's mind. This highlights the importance of being aware of the auditory environments we encounter, especially in places where we are constantly bombarded by sound, such as shopping malls, restaurants, and stores.

Food Addiction and DNA Degradation

The prevalence of mass programming has, no doubt, seeped into every aspect of your life, including your relationship with food. From the enticing advertisements bombarding you daily to the convenience of processed snacks readily available at every turn, you are constantly programmed to consume without considering the repercussions. However, beneath the surface lies a stark reality: food addiction, often laden with poisons, is not only detrimental to your physical health but also wreaks havoc on your genetic makeup.

Food addiction, subtly reinforced by mass programming, manifests in various forms, from cravings for sugary treats to the allure of highly processed, convenience foods. These cravings are not merely a matter of personal willpower but are deeply ingrained through years of exposure to marketing tactics and societal norms that promote indulgence and instant gratification. As a result, many people find themselves trapped in a cycle of overconsumption, leading to obesity, diabetes, and a myriad of other health issues.

What is even more alarming is the impact of these addictive, often toxic substances on your DNA. The poisons in your food, such as artificial additives, pesticides, and genetically modified organisms, have been shown to induce mutations and damage your genetic code. These alterations can disrupt vital cellular processes, impairing growth, development, overall well-being, and your evolution towards higher states of consciousness.

The degradation of your DNA doesn't just affect you but can also be passed down to future generations, perpetuating a cycle of genetic decline. Studies have already demonstrated the transgenerational effects of dietary toxins, highlighting the importance of breaking free from this harmful cycle for the sake of your descendants and the continuation of the species.

Breaking free from the grip of food addiction and the insidious influence of mass programming requires a concerted effort to reclaim your health and autonomy.

Breaking Free from Conditioned Responses

In essence, the prevalence of mass programming serves to perpetuate a state of collective ignorance and spiritual stagnation, hindering humanity's evolution towards higher levels of consciousness and understanding. Breaking free from these constraints necessitates a focused effort to question established narratives, explore alternative perspectives, and cultivate a deeper connection with your innate spiritual essence.

Embracing an inquisitive spirit is not a rejection of wisdom but a celebration of the human capacity to grow and evolve. When you challenge assumptions, the way is paved for new insights, deeper understanding, and the potential for transformative change.

For too long, humans as a collective have been told and taught to suppress their personal power and dim their own light to the point where so many remain uninformed, powerless, confused, and dependent on others, having forgotten who we are. You are encouraged to seek salvation, healing, wisdom, and knowledge outside of yourself to the point where you are no longer accountable for your own evolution and perhaps languor in being a victim of circumstances. Yet the seeds for activating the dormant DNA codes that will allow your neurological structure to expand can be awakened.

Remember, in the web of knowledge and beliefs that shape your understanding of the world, there lies a powerful invitation to question what you have been taught and told.

Re-Imagine
YOU

The power of an awakened mind lies in its ability to break the chains of mass control through awareness and knowledge. Within the beliefs and understandings that shape your perception of the world, there is a powerful invitation to question what you've been taught and told. Embracing a curious and inquisitive spirit is not a rejection of wisdom but a celebration of the human capacity to grow and evolve. By challenging assumptions, you pave the way for new insights, deeper understanding, and the potential for transformative change.

Through a process of questioning, you unearth gems of knowledge and discover the contours of your own convictions. Challenging the status quo unlocks the doors to progress and leads you to the power of discernment —finding and trusting your own truth. In a world where light can be deceptive, relying on the frequency of sound, which does not lie, becomes crucial. By listening to the truth in someone's voice, you can foster an authentic understanding that thus celebrates your capacity for growth and evolution.

1. **Awareness and Identification:**
   o   What are my core beliefs, and where did they originate?
   o   How much of my worldview is influenced by media, culture, and societal norms?
   o   Do I frequently conform to societal expectations without questioning them?

2. **Critical Thinking and Reflection:**
   o   When was the last time I questioned a widely accepted belief or norm?
   o   How do I handle information that contradicts my beliefs or values?
   o   What are my sources of information, and are they diverse and reliable?

3. **Personal Values and Authenticity:**
   o   What truly matters to me, and how does it align with my actions?
   o   Am I living a life true to my own values or someone else's expectations?
   o   In what ways do I compromise my authenticity to fit in or be accepted?

4. **Emotional and Psychological Freedom:**
   o   What fears or insecurities hold me back from expressing my true self?
   o   How do I respond to social pressure or criticism?
   o   What emotional triggers reveal areas where I might be conditioned?

"If the doors of perception were cleansed, all things would appear infinite."

William Blake

PART ONE
SUMMARY

- Dormant potential for ESP exists within every individual, with its activation regulated by the   functionality of the DNA. ESP is a normal attribute of the evolving human organism, as the consciousness contained within the body hologram continues its natural expansion into the greater portions of its evolutionary blueprint.
- The current presence of distortions and blockages within the DNA structure impedes and distorts the expression of ESP capabilities. These blockages stop your senses from fully connecting with higher-dimensional energies. These blockages are keeping you from fully experiencing the richer, deeper layers of reality around you.
- Whenever you respond or react without thinking, you are under the influence of a conditioned response, which makes them a powerful force in your life because they build your habits.
- When television is being watched, the brain's right hemisphere is twice as active as the left. The crossover from left to right actually releases a surge of the body's natural opiates – endorphins and enkephalins. Endorphins are structurally identical to opium and its derivatives, which include morphine, codeine, and even heroin, so that means TV works as a very efficient drug delivery system.
- The poisons present in your food induce mutations and damage to your genetic code. These alterations can disrupt vital cellular processes, impairing growth, development, overall well-being, and your evolution towards higher states of consciousness. Additionally, the degradation of your DNA can be passed down to future generations, perpetuating a cycle of genetic decline.

Dr. Carol Talbot

Re-Imagine **YOU**

Unveiling the BLUEPRINT:

Exploring the Origins and Multi-Dimensional Structure of Human DNA in Bioregenesis

Have you ever felt a deep, unshakable sense that you are far more than just a body—something beyond flesh, bone, and breath? Perhaps, at times, you've sensed another life calling to you from the shadows of your imagination, glimpsed an alternate reality where a single choice altered the entire course of your existence. What if, right now, in this very moment, another version of you is living a different life on a parallel timeline, where your dreams are realities, and the path not taken is unfolding? What if you could access the wisdom, experiences and power of all your possible selves existing across multiple dimensions? Is it truly possible?

As a child, I used to fly, soaring through vivid, exhilarating dreams. There was no weight to hold me down, no boundary to what I could do. And like many of us, the wonder of those dreams was slowly buried under the conditioning of the "real world." School, society, and the rules of everyday life pushed those experiences into the realm of fantasy. Yet deep within me, the knowledge that there was something more and something untouchable yet undeniably real remained. That seed of curiosity in my DNA whispered that I am so much more than I've been led to believe. And so are you.

The spark of curiosity that ignited my journey began in childhood when my mother introduced me to psychic artists, channeling sessions, and clairvoyants. Though some early experiences were more intimidating than enlightening, they unlocked a hunger to explore the unknown. Later in life, I discovered that this fascination with the esoteric was not just a fleeting interest but something embedded deep within my ancestral line. My grandfather, an avid reader of occult works by Madame Blavatsky and Alice Bailey, handed down an insatiable thirst for understanding the hidden truths of human potential.

My mother herself would secretly attend lectures in London to learn the teachings of Ouspensky, Gurdjieff, and other philosophers who dared to challenge the boundaries of reality. This was my inheritance - a lineage not just of blood but of untamed curiosity, a quest for knowledge that stretched back generations. And now, that quest has led me to the very blueprint of what makes us human - our DNA.

I've traveled the globe for decades, devouring wisdom from countless books, retreats, and mystical experiences. And now, the time has come to go beyond the veil, to lift the curtain on the greatest mystery of all: *who we really are.* Your DNA is more than a biological code; it's a multidimensional key, a gateway to other realms, ancient knowledge, and the limitless potential within you. It holds the secrets of your ancestors, the latent powers within your cells, and the divine blueprint of Source itself.

In the quiet moments of reflection, when I've dared to peer beyond the ordinary, I've realized that our DNA is not static, not fixed. It's alive, dynamic, evolving, and responsive. It holds the potential for bioregenesis, the ability to reawaken dormant strands and unlock the codes that connect you to higher realms of consciousness, other versions of yourself, and the universe itself. Within the intricate helixes of your DNA lies the wisdom of your ancestors, the lessons of alternate timelines, and the infinite potential you've yet to tap into.

So, I ask you: could it be that your true history, your multidimensional self, and the limitless potential of your existence are encoded within you, just waiting for the moment when you're ready to unlock it?

This is not just a journey of discovery. It's a revelation—a reimagining of what it means to be human.

Chapter Three

Source Consciousness,
The Physical Atomic Body Structure, Humanity, Matter & the Cosmos

KEY QUESTIONS:

Who are you?
What are you beyond the physical form?
What is a Source?
What is consciousness?

My earliest recollection of the idea of God came from being dutifully sent to the local village Methodist church every Sunday. Looking back, I suspect it had less to do with religious fervor and more with giving my parents a much-needed break from my brother and I. Still, those early experiences shaped a particular image of God—a towering, authoritative figure who, in just seven days, supposedly created everything we know. While I enjoyed the hymns and the community, especially during the Harvest Festival, there was always a lingering feeling of something *off* in the stories and sermons. Even as a child, I felt the pull to question what I was being told. Was this all there was to the grand mystery of existence?

Source Consciousness and the Infinite Field of Creation
Beyond the layers of cultural conditioning and the rigid concepts of God handed down through religion, a far more expansive and mind-

bending perspective began to emerge in my quest for answers. Quantum morphogenetic field physics proposes something truly awe-inspiring: an unquantifiable, limitless field of living, perpetual Source consciousness—the true origin of all creation, the pulse of life itself. This field is not some distant entity judging from the clouds but rather the living fabric of the cosmos, and guess what? You are part of it.

Imagine for a moment: at the heart of all existence lies an infinite wellspring of energy and consciousness, often called God, Source, Universal Mind, or Oneness. It's not a being in the sky but the pulsating rhythm of the universe, breathing in and out, creating and dissolving. Every particle, every star, every living being, including you, flows from this Source Point—a central command center of reality where all energy originates and returns. This essence connects everything, an eternal still point from which all life unfolds and to which it all returns. It's not something you can measure or define because the very act of trying to pin it down breaks the boundlessness that it truly is. It's the pulse of creation, beyond the reach of any religious doctrine, too vast and too magnificent to be confined to any singular story.

Here's the magic! Though you may not be able to know Source in its entirety directly, you can experience it through its creations, through life itself. It's like living in a holographic universe where every fragment, every moment, contains the blueprint of the whole. Imagine this, if you take a regular photograph and cut it in half, you're left with incomplete pieces. However, with a hologram, even when divided, every piece still contains the complete image of the original. That's what you are. Each person is a complete and perfect reflection of Source itself, eternally connected to the whole.

This is the boundless mystery of existence. The truth is, you are far more than you've been taught. You are not just a fragment of creation. You are a living, breathing embodiment of the entire cosmos.

There is nothing to compare Source to. It contains all time and no time. It contains everything and nothing at once, eternally, and it is limitless.

The Source Point is stillness, absence of motion, and often called the great void, yet it is all potential creation.

This Source Point is pure energy and can never be destroyed nor depleted, continually changing form through the rhythm of the cosmic matrix yet, at the same time, perpetually remaining the same. It will continually change form, although particle units never really change. It is simply the arrangement of particle units that gives the illusion of something instead of something else. Like a recipe, the ingredients are the same, and what you make from them differs.

In his book The Master Key, originally published as a 24-week correspondence course in 1912, author Charles F. Haanel states, "The Universal Mind is static or potential energy; it simply is. It can manifest only through the individual, and the individua can manifest only through the Universal. They are one."

Everything that will ever exist, exists in a state of potential creation. In other words, Source perpetuates itself through an eternal act of fusion and fission, like switching a light on and off. You are an active part of creation. You are a Creator within creation and taking place within.

A true human is a part of an incredibly structured and ordered Cosmos created by intention and purpose. The physical body is just one aspect, and you exist far beyond the form of only physical expression. In fact, only a small part of your expression and consciousness is stationed within that which is known as the body. In fact, all people exist as individualized embodiments of a greater energy identity.

This greater identity can be viewed as the portion of your conscious awareness that is too large in energy volume to fit into the limited confines of the body structure. The body and the consciousness focused within it exist within this greater pool of energy, and it is this energy that creates the body, sets the autonomic body processes, and continually feeds the body life force energy.

The Blueprint of All Matter and Consciousness

The fundamental connection between humanity, matter, and the Cosmos is established through Morphogenetic Fields, which can be described as the fabric of creation. These fields consist of conscious sound and light templates, serving as the fundamental blueprints upon which matter and conscious identity can materialize. This phenomenon occurs both on a microcosmic and macrocosmic scale.

Morphogenetic fields can be compared to the invisible design grid architects use to create blueprints for buildings. Imagine the universe as a grand architectural project, where these design grids are not just on paper but woven into the fabric of existence.

These grids, made up of light and sound, serve as the underlying templates or blueprints. Just as an architect's grid helps translate design ideas into physical structures, morphogenetic fields guide the formation of both matter and consciousness.

At the macrocosmic level, the universe itself is a vast field of consciousness that encompasses and contains all other forms of reality and manifestation. It can be conceptualized as 'all that is,' the expansive stage upon which experiential reality unfolds.

Within this vast expanse of 'all that is' lie the blueprints for every conceivable thing and identity, continuously created and renewed. The cosmic order serves as the foundation for human order, with experiential reality fields emerging from energy templates grouped into specific patterns and arrangements that form the morphogenetic structure and blueprint for all dimensions.

The Structure of Reality

In this context, dimensions are defined as fixed groupings of energy organized within geometrically arranged forms constructed upon crystallized conscious units of sound and light.

Imagine dimensions as different floors in a skyscraper. Each floor is like a unique level of reality, constructed with its own design and layout.

These floors are built using special building blocks made of sound and light, like the bricks and mortar that form the structure. Just as each floor has its own purpose and arrangement, each dimension is a distinct realm of energy organized in a specific geometric pattern.

When you delve into the underlying order of energy from which manifest reality emerges, you essentially explore the intricate mechanics and dynamics of dimensionalized morphogenetic fields in which conscious experience unfolds.

The true power of a human being as a spiritual creation exists in realms of anatomy that are beyond what is seen in three-dimensional form. These areas of your anatomy directly direct what your physical atomic body will do. They direct the birth, aging, and growth processes, and they direct whether you will be healthy or sick. In other words, multi-dimensional anatomy has not been used for thousands of years.

By grasping this multi-dimensional anatomy, you not only unlock the secrets to awakening your intron DNA and accessing Higher Sensory Perception but also gain insight into the nature of your Spirit Body— often referred to as your consciousness—which serves as the foundational grid template for your physical form. Understanding this connection reveals how any issues in the template can manifest as physical challenges.

The way your system works is that when you are in spirit form, you enter a process called fetal integration, where you, as spirit consciousness, come into a body vehicle to have an incarnation here in this 'game' or reality field. However, there is a challenge with the body pattern because of template distortions. As soon as consciousness intertwines with the physical atomic body and the DNA template, approximately 90% of your consciousness is shut off. This disconnect means you no longer remember who you truly are or your cosmic history. Like a light switch dimming most of its current, the body restricts the flow of consciousness, limiting your ability to bring through the memory of yourself as a multi-dimensional being.

Now, imagine the potential that awaits you if your DNA could be refined and repaired, unlocking the full extent of your consciousness and allowing you to rediscover your true essence. This is similar to the narrative in the movie *Lucy*, where Lucy's transformation begins when a synthetic substance called CPH4 enters her system. Initially meant for different purposes, this substance invades her bloodstream, unlocking her cognitive faculties in ways she could never have imagined.

As the CPH4 takes effect, Lucy experiences an exponential expansion in her mental capabilities, challenging the conventional belief that humans only use a small percentage of their brains. Her mind opens to new dimensions, granting her heightened sensory perception, telekinetic abilities, and control over time itself. Lucy's journey represents the dramatic potential lying dormant within us and the idea that, with the right trigger, we can unlock extraordinary abilities far beyond what we perceive as possible.

Just as Lucy's encounter with CPH4 unlocks her full cognitive potential, imagine the possibilities as your DNA undergoes a similar refinement, allowing you to elevate your consciousness and reclaim your true multidimensional nature. If fully embodied with the true human template, you would have access to at least 12 dimensions of consciousness far beyond the limitations of your current three-dimensional existence. Like the Masters and Gurus described in Baird T. Spalding's series of books, you too could move through these multidimensional realms, not just in consciousness but also physically, becoming a fully realized being able to transcend space, time, and reality.

Imagine a grand, ancient library with 12 floors. Each floor represents a different level of knowledge, understanding, and experience. The first floor is easily accessible, filled with everyday information that everyone can understand. As you ascend to higher floors, the knowledge becomes more specialized, profound, and complex, requiring a deeper level of awareness and understanding to access.

To access these higher floors, you need special keys. Each key represents a new level of consciousness or personal development. As you gather these keys, you unlock the ability to move up to the next floor, gaining access to richer, more intricate knowledge and experiences.

Just as each library floor offers new knowledge that builds upon what came before, each dimension in this metaphor represents a deeper level of reality, unlocking greater wisdom with every key you collect.

As you delve into the concept of multi-dimensional identity and human design, it's crucial to recognize that your current understanding of DNA and human existence is limited. To truly grasp the complexity of your design, you must embrace a multi-dimensional reality model that acknowledges Earth and the universe as part of a larger harmonic structure. This perspective reveals that the original human design originated from higher dimensional systems, existing within other harmonics of matter beyond your current perception.

Multi-Dimensional Identity & Human Design

Modern science has only scratched the surface of understanding the true function and structure of human DNA, and it knows even less about the original design of humanity. A profound realization unfolds when you begin to embrace a multi-dimensional reality model, recognizing that Earth and the universe represent just one harmonic of matter density. This awareness opens the door to the existence of other universes within different dimensions and harmonics of matter. It suggests that the original blueprint of humanity was not solely confined to this reality but emerged from 'otherworldly' systems, originating in higher-dimensional realms and harmonics of matter.

A way to understand this is to imagine human DNA as a complex, multi-layered symphony. Modern science is like a group of musicians who can only hear and play a few notes on their instruments. They are skilled in their craft but unaware that the symphony extends far beyond the notes they know. To truly understand the entire symphony, these musicians need to recognize that their instruments are part of a grand orchestra playing a harmony that includes sounds and dimensions they have yet to discover. Similarly, human DNA and design are part of a greater cosmic orchestra, with origins and functions rooted in higher dimensional harmonics that go beyond our current scientific understanding.

Just as this symphony of human DNA involves layers and harmonics extending beyond current understanding, so does the very fabric of reality itself.

Everything in existence is composed of consciousness, and the solidity you perceive is the result of the interaction between the consciousness observing the form and the consciousness that constitutes it.

Human consciousness emerges through a sequence of dimensions that create a framework within which the interconnection of consciousness can transpire. Your observation of solidness and materialization is determined by the oscillation rates between the dimensionality of the units of consciousness, which generate energy frequencies. The human consciousness and physical form are frequency patterns designed by the dimensionality of the units of consciousness.

Returning to the analogy of an orchestra, we consider human consciousness a symphony orchestra. Each instrument represents a dimension of consciousness, and together, they create a harmonious framework for the interconnection of consciousness.

Now, let's focus on the music produced by this orchestra. The melody and rhythm are determined by how fast or slow each instrument plays, comparable to the oscillation rates between the dimensions of consciousness. These oscillation rates generate frequencies of energy, much like different musical notes.

The human consciousness and physical form are like specific musical compositions or patterns created by the interplay of these frequencies. Just as a composer designs a piece of music by arranging different notes and rhythms, the dimensionality of the units of consciousness designs the pattern of human consciousness and physical form through their frequencies.

As the dimensional frequencies shape the patterns of human consciousness and form, how you perceive reality is influenced by your position within these frequency bands, and you perceive dense and solid dimensions that exist just below the frequency of your consciousness.

This perception is rooted in the broader process called 'Vibrational Down-stepping.' Everything in existence, manifest and unmanifest, originates from pure Source consciousness, which dimensionalizes itself into distinct forms to experience reality within the space-time-matter framework.

The Multi-Dimensional Anatomy of Human Beings

Every being and thing in any manifest reality field comes into being through this process. In relation to the human form, the structure of dimensionalized consciousness takes the form of the 15 dimensional identities of the time matrix structure.

The 15 dimensional time matrix exists within the Source field. It's how consciousness structures itself for the experience of being known.

Planet Earth exists in one of the countless energetic structures called 15 dimensional time matrices. Many energy-time matrices follow a specific mathematical, geometrical program through which consciousness can experience space, time and matter based on the time matrix structure.

Harmonic Universes and the Human Template

Within one matrix are 15 dimensions arranged into sets of three dimensional reality fields. Each set of three is called a 'Harmonic Universe' or 'Density Level.' Each Harmonic Universe represents a level of matter density specific to its fundamental rate of vibration and oscillation. Each frequency dimension also has 12 sub-frequency bands, and Earth exists within one of the Harmonic Universes.

It's all consciousness, but consciousness occupies space and time in different time-space coordinates.

Since a dimension is a frequency, and a frequency band is a rhythm of vibration and oscillation, the only thing distinguishing one dimension from another is the rate of vibration and oscillation.

The greater the vibration, or more density, the denser consciousness. Each dimension has certain sets of laws and principles specific to that dimension's frequency. Those who resonate with a particular energy level, referring to their vibration and light quotient, exist in that dimension.

If you consider water, it exists in three states - water, ice, and steam. The difference is the rate at which the molecules are moving. Ice is water slowed down, and steam is water speeded up. They are simply different states that water can assume.

So, dimensions are just different states of being.

Human design is a multi-dimensional network of conscious energy structures intricately connected within a Cosmic System, each mirroring the other. The ancient Hermetic principle, "as above, so below," accurately illustrates that the human system is deeply intertwined with the cosmic order. Your human identity emerges as a projection of consciousness originating from Source Consciousness.

The physical human body emerges into manifestation and materialization because of intricate, multidimensional dynamics of light and sound. This is the basis of the true secrets of physical materialization. All manifest forms, including biological systems, emerge into physical materialization through a complex system of energetic structures that span the sets of 15 dimensional frequency bands upon which multidimensional reality fields are ordered. The physically manifest aspects of the human body represent only one small portion of the true human anatomy.

The blueprint of human consciousness mirrors the structure of all dimensional systems. It is divided into five groups of three dimensions, forming distinct yet interconnected morphogenetic bodies composed of light and sound, within which various aspects of consciousness are housed. The five dimensionalized bodies of human anatomy represent distinct portions of identity and awareness that manifest 'in time' (see diagram 1).

	Harmonic Universe 1	Harmonic Universe 2	Harmonic Universe 3	Harmonic Universe 4	Harmonic Universe 5
Dimensions	1, 2, 3	4, 5, 6	7,8,9	10,11,12	13,14, 15 (known as the primal light fields)
Type of Biology	Gross Physical Matter, carbon-based biology	Physical matter, carbon-silica biology	Etheric Matter, silica-based biology	Pre-matter – hydroplasmic liquid light	Ante-matter – thermos-plasmic light
Identity	Incarnate self	Soul self	Oversoul self	Avatar or Christos Self	Rishi or Higher Self

(Diagram 1)

Each has multiple expressions of identity in which singular identities and biologies are created. The five dimensionalized bodies are storehouses of all human consciousness. However, conscious physical identity itself is primarily locked into dimension 3, intuitive identity in dimension 2, and subconscious identity in lower dimension 2 and dimension 1. The dimensions act as frequency bands where portions of your multi-dimensional identity are stationed. In humans, these levels of Self or expression are called:

- Incarnate – stationed in Dimension 1,2 and 3 or Harmonic Universe One
- Soul – stationed in Dimension 4, 5, and 6 or Harmonic Universe Two
- Oversoul – stationed in Dimension 7, 8, and 9 or Harmonic Universe Three
- Christos or Avatar – stationed in Dimension 10, 11, and 12 or Harmonic Universe Four
- Rishi or Monad – stationed in Dimension 13, 14, and 15 or Harmonic Universe Five

Similarly, there are expressions of this Earth at each Density level or Harmonic Universe:

- In Harmonic Universe One, it is called Earth
- In Harmonic Universe Two, it is called Tara
- In Harmonic Universe Three, it is called Gaia
- In Harmonic Universe Four, it is called Aramatena

Each of the levels of Self in each Harmonic Universe has a characteristic quality that results in a matter form that is unique to each Harmonic Universe. For example, in Harmonic Universe One, matter forms are primarily carbon-based, while those in Harmonic Universe Two are both carbon and silica-based. Those in Harmonic Universe four are liquid, principally light, and in Harmonic Universe five, units of consciousness do not manifest into matter or biological forms and, for this reason, are referred to as pre-matter. Harmonic Universe Five, also known as the Primal Light Field, contains Collective Groups of Consciousness of Source that form the biological forms within Harmonic Universes one to four.

Stairstep Creation & Vibrational Down-Stepping

The creation process begins with Source sub-dividing itself to create smaller, simultaneous versions of itself, each experiencing different aspects of creation. This process, known as Stairstep Creation, occurs in groupings of twelves based on the geometrical matrix of space and time.

Source first projects its consciousness into the 15th, 14th, and 13th dimensions of Harmonic Universe 5, forming 12 Rishi or Monadic identities (collectives of consciousness). These Rishi identities exist beyond the constraints of time and represent the realm of true ascended masters. From there, the Rishi consciousness divides further, projecting 12 portions of itself into the 12th, 11th, and 10th dimensions of Harmonic Universe 4, giving rise to the pre-matter liquid light Avatar collectives.

The Avatar collectives, in turn, project 12 portions of their consciousness into the 9th, 8th, and 7th dimensions of Harmonic Universe 3, forming the morphogenetic fields that shape etheric matter and silica-based life forms of the Oversoul collectives. These Oversoul collectives then project

12 portions into the 6th, 5th, and 4th dimensions of Harmonic Universe 2, creating the Soul collectives.

Finally, the Soul collectives project 12 portions of their consciousness into the 3rd, 2nd, and 1st dimensions of Harmonic Universe 1, where morphogenetic templates form the basis for gross matter and carbon-based life forms of the Incarnate collectives. This process underpins the individual morphogenetic structures that shape all life in this realm.

Alternate Realities and Multiple Timelines

The concept of "probable selves" also hinges on the idea that every decision spawns alternate realities where different choices are made. Imagine your life as a vast tree with countless branches. Each branch represents a path your life could take, diverging from the main trunk whenever you decide.

In this framework, every choice creates a new branch, a new reality where an alternate version of you, a probable self, lives out the consequences of that choice. These branches aren't just metaphorical; they represent fully realized alternate worlds, each as real as the one you perceive yourself to be living in now.

This idea suggests that for every "you" who made a particular decision, there exists another "you" who made a different choice, thus experiencing an entirely different life trajectory. These probable selves explore the vast landscape of potential futures, each contributing to the richness of the overall human experience.

The series "Dark Matter" on Apple TV, based on Blake Crouch's novel, delves into this concept by exploring the life of a physicist who stumbles into a multiverse, encountering different versions of himself. Each version has lived a different life based on various decisions, embodying the notion that your choices shape your realities in profound and diverse ways.

In this multiverse, the protagonist's journey highlights the interconnectedness of all these alternate realities, suggesting that your probable selves are not isolated but part of a larger, intricate web of existence.

Within this step-down sequence lie the secrets and processes for your evolution as you marvel at the sheer enormity of the magnificent step-down process from Source and the pathway back to Source to which you are always connected. Through understanding this hierarchy of identities from which you emerge, you gain a more expansive view of your true nature and the pathway of evolution. Since all existence occurs in the same space, your evolution requires a shift in raising and lowering oscillation and vibratory rates rather than the dated view of moving to another place or space!

Remember, within the gift of your creation, the goal is to achieve multi-dimensional identity integration. Many other identities are you and more expanded self-realized parts of yourself. The journey is to know yourself and to become more of who you truly are.

The Threat of Disconnection from the True Soul Matrix

Your fourth, fifth, and sixth-dimensional identities are known as the soul matrix. Certain structures, including your DNA, link the body, mind, and emotions to this soul matrix of energy. It is possible to manipulate the subtle energy bodies, splice an individual from one soul matrix into another matrix, and disconnect the bio-energetic circuitry from the original soul. Interestingly, in Philip Pullman's televised series, "His Dark Materials," the concept of splicing an individual from their soul matrix is a pivotal aspect of the story.

While this process can assist individuals under certain conditions, it can also disable individuals from connecting with their greater identity and innate spiritual connection. This is precisely what certain digressed races have in mind as part of their agenda. Linking those selected from the human populace into a false matrix allows humans to be easily controlled. The false matrix continually projects certain holographic inserts, making them appear as permanent reality features. Any sensually illusional reality could be sustained in such a way, and the humans involved would have no idea or memory indicating that anything was out of order.

For example, consider a city where every citizen wears augmented reality (AR) glasses that project an overlay onto the world. This overlay is so seamless and sophisticated that it becomes indistinguishable from the real world. Through these AR glasses, the city's environment, the appearance of people, and even the flow of events are subtly manipulated.

Now, consider that this AR system is controlled by an unseen entity, projecting specific holographic inserts designed to shape the citizens' perceptions and behaviors. The entity uses these inserts to create the illusion of a perfect, harmonious society where everyone is content and everything functions smoothly.

For example, if a street has become unsafe or unsightly, the AR system projects a beautiful park instead. Seeing the park through their AR glasses, the citizens stroll through it happily, unaware of the reality hidden behind the projection. Similarly, if there's political unrest or social conflict, the AR system might project scenes of peace and cooperation, ensuring that the citizens continue to believe in the stability and harmony of their society.

In this scenario, the holographic inserts are so deeply integrated into the citizens' daily experiences that they accept them as permanent features of their reality. The citizens have no memory or awareness of any discrepancy because the AR system continuously updates their perceptions, erasing any traces of the true reality that might otherwise cause doubt or confusion.

This highlights how a sensually illusional reality can be sustained indefinitely, with the people involved having no idea that their perceptions are being controlled.

As the individual becomes disconnected from their original soul matrix, all memory contained within its DNA and cellular memory is wiped away, and the soul matrix acts as the programming device and storage house for human memory. When the human is fully connected to the false matrix, the original connection to the soul can then be disengaged, and the new matrix will program the DNA and download the memories purposely programmed into the false matrix.

At this point in the process, there would be a brief lapse of all memory and a minor disability in short-term memory functions while the cellular code processes its new set of instructions. Pieces of memory from the old program may emerge spontaneously from cellular residue and interface with the operational instructions from the new program, distorting the electrical impulse patterns to the brain and the chemical balances of human biology.

Like humans, planets and galaxies also possess a soul matrix, of which the soul matrices of all the system inhabitants are a part.

Scientists have labeled 'junk DNA' a portion of the disassembled codes from our original soul matrices. This so-called 'junk' is part of the heritage that holds the potential to lead you back to the wholeness of your true identity. The key codes of access removed and placed in storage backup keep you separated from the base imprint of your DNA (and out of your perceptual range) by the employment of a Frequency Fence. This has created a barrier in minute sound particles that have kept your base DNA from picking up the contents of the stored electrified sound signals.

Manipulating Reality Through Frequency

A Frequency Fence is a technology possessed by those with a working understanding of universal physics. By manipulating sound wave patterns and cycles, many things can be created, for the energy identified as sound serves as the glue that holds together matter patterns within the time matrix. It is sound that directs matter, and thus, anything cloaked in matter can be directly influenced by sound.

Preston B. Nichols talks about encoding thought forms into music and calls this electromagnetic telepathy in his book, The Music of Time. Consider that your reality or reference frame for consciousness is based purely on sounds, notes, and tones, and all these aspects are frequencies. In fact, every physical object or manifestation you can conceive of conforms to a frequency or can be identified as having a specific frequency. By playing with certain frequencies, riots or raucous behavior can be induced. Conversely, a wild crowd can be subdued by the same methods.

An innovative Russian team discovered that living human DNA can be changed and rearranged with sound using spoken words and phrases. They found that the key to changing DNA with words and phrases lies in using the right frequency. For example, a research team successfully transmitted information patterns from one set of DNA to another. Eventually, they could even reprogram cells to another genome, transforming frog embryos into salamander embryos without lifting a single scalpel or making one incision. This way, all information was transmitted without any side effects or disharmonies encountered when cutting out and re-introducing single genes from the DNA.

It is important to note that human DNA functions within a very specific pattern of frequency. This frequency directs all the body's processes and significantly shapes the type and range of perception experienced through that biological organism. Your sensory perception is intricately tied to the limited spectrum of frequencies you can perceive. For instance, in the realm of sight, humans can only perceive a small range of electromagnetic waves as visible light, while vast portions of the spectrum, such as infrared and ultraviolet, remain invisible. Similarly, in the hearing domain, you are tuned to a narrow bandwidth of sound frequencies, missing out on sonic information present in the broader spectrum of sound waves. Thus, your understanding of the world is inherently constrained by the limited frequencies your sensory organs can detect, highlighting the fascinating interplay between biology and perception. Furthermore, this means that to direct the focus of human perception, a knowledge of sound genetics is required.

Ultimately, manipulating reality through frequency is not just a theory but a profound truth woven into the fabric of existence. Sound, as the glue that binds matter, is key to altering the structures around us and the DNA that defines us. As research continues to uncover how frequencies can reprogram cells and reshape life, it becomes clear that the limitations of human perception are not permanent barriers but thresholds waiting to be expanded.

Imagine the possibilities when you consciously harness this knowledge to heal and evolve yourself and shift the reality you inhabit. Just as sound frequencies can shape DNA and perception, they can also be used to expand your awareness beyond the narrow confines of what you currently experience. With a deeper understanding of sound genetics and frequency manipulation, you can tap into the untold potential of human consciousness—unlocking new dimensions of reality, new states of being, and, perhaps, rediscovering the boundless nature of who you truly are.

The question remains. Are you ready to tune in and play your part in this cosmic orchestra?

Re-Imagine
YOU

I invite you to expand your awareness and fully consider the following questions. You may wish to pre-record the questions, leaving at least 2 minutes between them and utilizing them as a meditation, sitting or lying in a comfortable position with your eyes closed.

1. Who are you?
2. Who wouldn't you be if you weren't you?
3. What wouldn't you be if you weren't you?
4. What wouldn't it be like not to be you?
5. Where wouldn't you be if you weren't here?
6. Who are you now?

Let these questions guide you to deeper layers of self-awareness and understanding, opening pathways to greater insight into your true nature.

Quantum Jumping Meditation

Preparation:

1. Find a quiet, comfortable space where you won't be disturbed.
2. Sit or lie down in a relaxed position.
3. Close your eyes and take a few deep breaths, inhaling deeply through your nose and exhaling slowly through your mouth.

Step-by-Step Guide:

- Grounding:
  - o Visualize roots extending from the base of your spine or the soles of your feet into the Earth. Imagine these roots going deep into the Earth, anchoring you firmly.

- o Feel the stability and support of the Earth, drawing energy up through these roots into your body.
- ◉ **Creating Your Quantum Space:**
  - o Imagine standing in front of a large, ornate mirror. This mirror is not just any mirror; it is a portal to other dimensions and realities.
  - o See your reflection in the mirror and acknowledge yourself in this moment, grounding your current awareness.
- ◉ **Stepping Through the Mirror:**
  - o When ready, take a deep breath and step through the mirror. Feel yourself moving through a membrane, transitioning into a different realm.
  - o On the other side of the mirror, find yourself in a vast, open space filled with swirling energies and infinite possibilities. This is your Quantum Space, a place where all your probable selves exist.
- ◉ **Meeting Your Probable Selves:**
  - o In this Quantum Space, call forth a probable self who has made a different decision or taken a different path in life. This self is an aspect of you living a different reality.
  - o See this probable self-approaching you. Observe their appearance, energy, and demeanor. They may look similar to you or quite different.
- ◉ **Interacting with Your Probable Self:**
  - o Engage in a dialogue with your probable self. Ask them about their life, experiences, and the decisions they made that led them to this reality.
  - o Listen attentively to their insights and wisdom. You can ask for guidance, share your experiences, and learn from their perspectives.
- ◉ **Exploring Other Probable Selves:**
  - o Repeat the process with other probable selves, exploring different realities and timelines. Each interaction broadens

your perspective and deepens your multi-dimensional awareness.

- ⊙ **Returning to Your Present Reality:**
  - o When you feel complete, thank your probable selves for their insights and bid them farewell.
  - o Step back through the mirror, returning to your present reality. Feel yourself grounding back into your physical body, bringing with you the expanded awareness and knowledge you have gained.
- ⊙ **Reflection:**
  - o Take a moment to reflect on your experiences. Journal any insights, emotions, or sensations that arose during the meditation.
  - o Notice how your expanded awareness influences your perception of your current reality.
- ⊙ **Closing:**
  - o Take a few deep breaths, wiggling your fingers and toes to ground yourself into the present moment.
  - o When you feel ready, open your eyes and take a moment to appreciate the expanded awareness and multi-dimensional understanding you have cultivated.

This Quantum Jumping Meditation allows you to actively engage with your probable selves, explore different realities, and integrate their wisdom into your current life, offering a powerful and transformative experience.

"Within each of us lies a universe of infinite potential, where every possibility and every path coexist, awaiting our conscious exploration and choice. We are not just a single existence, but a vast tapestry of interconnected dimensions and realities, each reflecting the boundless nature of our true essence."'

Re-Imagine **YOU**

Chapter Four
The Basis of DNA —
the building blocks of life

KEY QUESTIONS:

What exactly is DNA?
Why is it so important to repair your DNA?
What does DNA have to do with aging and longevity?

Have you ever wondered, "Where did humans come from?" "How did it all begin?" or "Is there truly a beginning?" And if there is a beginning, does that mean there must be an end?

While we often think of time as moving from the past to the present and then into the future, it's actually more accurate to understand time as flowing from the future into the present and then into the past.

In every present moment, you are constantly creating and imagining what you desire to experience or achieve in the future. This vision of the future acts as a guide, influencing your thoughts, actions, and decisions in the now. As you take action in the present, those future possibilities manifest and take form, becoming your current reality. Once experienced, they are stored as memories, gradually becoming the past.

This perspective of time flowing from the future through the present and into the past is essential because it emphasizes that the future is not something distant and fixed but a living potential shaped by your current intentions and choices. As time unfolds, the future you envision becomes the present moment, and eventually, it recedes into the past.

Understanding this flow of time also links intriguingly to the evolution of life. Just as your actions in the present shape your future and become your past, the traits and behaviors of a species evolve over time through adaptation. Much like time, evolution is a continuous process of creation, experience, and memory, where the future holds the potential for new forms of life, which eventually solidify into the present and become part of history.

Transitioning into Darwin's evolutionary theory, a parallel can be seen in how ongoing processes of selection and adaptation shape both individual lives and the development of a species. Exploring Darwin's idea of natural selection, you can see how advantageous traits are passed down through generations, leading to the gradual evolution of a species over time—much like how your present intentions shape your future experiences and eventually become part of your past.

Contrary to this evolutionary theory, an alternative perspective suggests that humans may have evolved or been created through a different process. The work of molecular biologists Francis Crick and Leslie Orgel supports this idea.

The Cosmic Origin of Humanity

Imagine a time long before recorded history, where civilizations of extraordinary humans roamed the Earth—beings with capabilities and genetic superiority far beyond what is known today. These ancient humans, as described in Ashayana Deane's *Voyagers* series, were not merely products of Earth but cosmic hybrids. Their DNA was a mixture of genetic materials gathered from across the galaxy, infused with the wisdom and power of the stars. They lived in harmony with advanced civilizations from other worlds, beings who seeded their knowledge and essence into the fabric of early human life.

What if your very DNA holds remnants of this cosmic heritage?

The provocative theory put forth by William Bramley in *The Gods of Eden* suggests that life on Earth might have been deliberately spread across space and seeded intentionally by advanced intelligence. Picture this, civilizations far older than Earth, mastering the art of creation, deciding to plant the seeds of life on this planet. They didn't leave it to chance. Instead, they guided the process, ensuring that life would flourish in worlds like ours, an intentional act of cosmic gardening.

Consider the bold ideas of Zecharia Sitchin, who believed that our creation was not entirely natural but the result of deliberate genetic manipulation by advanced beings—the Anunnaki. According to Sitchin, these beings played a pivotal role in the creation of early humans, but they didn't give us everything. They held back the keys to health, longevity, and immortality—elements that were part of the original design for humanity.

The idea that extraterrestrial hands shaped our evolution suggests that we, as humans, are far more than we appear. We are diminished versions of what we were meant to be, with untapped potential lying dormant in our very DNA, waiting to be awakened.

Could the blueprint for your true potential lie in your genetic code, a legacy of cosmic origins that stretch far beyond Earth? And if so, what might happen if you could access the full spectrum of your ancestral power?

In *Voyagers 1*, it is suggested that the true origins of humanity lie in a fifth-dimensional counterpart of Earth, known as Tara. The original human prototype was created with genetic material from several advanced star groups, including the Zionites. Far from being ordinary beings, humans were initially designed to be the custodians and guardians of Tara, deeply connected to the cosmos. They engaged freely in intergalactic and interdimensional exchanges with various civilizations, standing as stewards of this higher-dimensional world.

De-Evolution & The Fragmentation of the 12-Strand DNA Blueprint

Over time, humanity began to fall into a state of de-evolution. What was once a species designed with the ability to access higher dimensions and knowledge became trapped in cycles of genetic distortion and misuse of power. The original human prototype, known as the Turaneusiam, began to lose its connection to its source, and this decline in genetic integrity led to a profound shift in the human experience, marked by confusion, imbalance, and regression.

As the planet Tara, humanity's fifth-dimensional home, underwent cycles of magnetic realignment and rebalancing, the creators of the Turaneusiam knew that a new path was needed. To prevent the complete collapse of this once-magnificent species, they made a bold decision: humanity would be seeded into the Earth system once more, but this time, with a more gradual process of evolution.

This process involved fragmenting the original human genetic blueprint, which was designed with 12 fully active DNA strands into twelve distinct units. Each of these 12 strands was separated and polarized, embedded into different sub-species. Each group was tasked with a unique evolutionary challenge - to overcome the duality encoded into their strand of DNA. This was no simple process. These polarized strands contained aspects of light and shadow, and only through mastery of both could these groups reunite their divided DNA into one complete and unified strand.

As each group successfully integrated and balanced its polarized DNA, it would then merge with the other groups who had done the same, gradually restoring the full 12-strand blueprint of the original human prototype. This genetic re-bundling was not just about survival but about reclaiming the potential for higher consciousness, interdimensional awareness, and the guardianship role humanity was originally designed to fulfill. However, this intricate and long-term plan was fragile and designed to take hundreds of thousands of years. If humanity could evolve and heal the distortions within its genetic makeup, the species would eventually regain its original potential. Bu⁻ if not, de-evolution would continue, and the human race would once again risk losing its place in the grand cosmic design.

This evolutionary journey is not without resistance. Powerful forces, both interdimensional and within the Earth system, have long sought to exploit the human species and the energy grids of Earth and Tara. If humanity succeeds in restoring its original DNA blueprint, the balance of power would shift, and Earth, along with other realms, would no longer be free for exploitation. The stakes are high—not just for humanity but for the entire cosmos.

DNA, the blueprint of life itself, is at the core of this epic struggle. These 12 strands hold the keys to higher perception, the ability to traverse dimensions, and the wisdom encoded in the original human design. Understanding this cosmic plan reveals not just the intricacies of DNA but the incredible potential locked within every human being. Will we evolve and unlock the full spectrum of our potential, or will we again fall into de-evolution and forget who we truly are? The answer lies within our DNA and our ability to rise beyond the forces that would see us fail.

Delving deeper into the intricate workings of the human blueprint and the cosmic forces at play, it's essential first to grasp the fundamental essence of your biological makeup. Transitioning from the cosmic narrative to the intricacies of life's building blocks, let's explore the basics of DNA, a molecule that holds the keys to your existence.

The Basics of DNA & The Original Human Blueprint

Deoxyribonucleic acid (DNA) contains genetic instructions for the development and function of living things. DNA is like a set of instructions. Instead of building machines, houses, or gadgets, it builds living things like you. All known cellular life and some viruses contain DNA. According to science, the main role of DNA in the cell is long-term information storage.

Imagine DNA as a super-long and twisting ladder or spiral staircase inside your cells. It is made up of tiny building blocks called nucleotides, currently identified as adenine, guanine, cytosine, thymine, and uracil, which have the symbols A, G, C, T, and U. These nucleotides are like letters in an alphabet, with each letter or nucleotide carrying a specific code that tells your body how to grow, what color your eyes will be and even what diseases you could be prone to. DNA contains the instructions for an organism to develop, survive, and reproduce. To carry out these functions, DNA sequences must be converted into messages that can be used to produce proteins, which are the complex molecules that do most of the work in your body.

DNA works as an interpreter and transmitter of frequency, energy, and consciousness. It works the same way a piece of film does. When the projector's light passes through the film, you project the picture or the movie onto the screen. DNA is what you use to process consciousness. It's a consciousness processor, transmitter, and translator. In fact, you cannot translate frequency without the use of DNA.

To summarize:

- Film Projector – your body
- Film strip – your DNA
- Light – your consciousness
- Screen – your reality

Your DNA acts as the vessel through which your physical, external reality is manufactured. Your external reality is the screen upon which thought forms stored within your cellular memory program can be displayed. DNA operates as the electromagnetic circuitry through which that memory comes into perceptual manifestation. The state of your DNA plays a crucial role in the holographic reality you manifest and materialize. Distortions in your DNA create distortions in your manifest reality, affecting your physical, mental, emotional, and spiritual well-being. Therefore, it is essential to address the state of your DNA to ensure a harmonious and coherent experience of reality.

The Phantom DNA Effect

Researchers, such as Dr. Glen Rein, have proposed that DNA can act as a receiver and transmitter of electromagnetic signals. Still, it might also involve accessing non-local information. Non-local information refers to data not confined to a specific location; it's a concept often associated with psychic phenomena like clairvoyance. In his study titled 'Consciousness and the New Biology of DNA, Rein discusses the potential of DNA to influence consciousness and the possibility of DNA acting as an antenna for external fields. Just like a radio antenna picks up music and talk shows from the airwaves, your DNA might pick up and transmit energy signals from the environment. These signals could be anything from light and sound to more mysterious forms of energy.

This idea opens exciting possibilities. If your DNA can interact with these energy fields, it might help explain some psychic abilities, like knowing things without being told (clairvoyance). It also means that taking care of your DNA could improve your physical, mental, and emotional well-being.

Several examples can illustrate the concept of DNA acting as an antenna for external fields and accessing non-local information:

The Phantom DNA Effect: In the 1990s, Russian scientists led by Dr. Vladimir Poponin conducted experiments that seemed to suggest that DNA can affect the quantum field. They observed that when DNA was placed in a vacuum, it appeared to cause a measurable structuring of the surrounding photons, which remained even after the DNA was removed. Some have interpreted this as evidence that DNA can interact with and influence non-local energy fields.

Think of times when you walk into a room and immediately sense a certain "vibe," whether it's a calm, happy, or tense atmosphere. This could be similar to how DNA interacts with the quantum field. If your DNA is sensitive to subtle energy fields, it might explain why you pick up on the mood of a place or people, even when no one has said a word. It could also help explain those moments when you "feel" a loved one's presence or emotion from a distance, suggesting that your DNA can connect to non-local energy fields.

The Global Consciousness Project: This project, initiated by Dr. Roger Nelson at Princeton University, aimed at exploring the idea that collective human consciousness can interact with and influence random number generators (RNGs) worldwide. While not directly related to DNA, the project supports the idea that consciousness and biological systems may interact with external energy fields, potentially pointing to a non-local connection that DNA could also be part of.

Have you ever noticed how certain events, like a major global celebration or a tragedy, seem to create a shared emotional experience? For instance, during major global events like the Olympics or crises, many people worldwide seem to "tune in" to the same emotional wavelength. If collective consciousness can influence physical systems like random number generators, as the project suggests, it means that your individual thoughts and emotions might contribute to a larger field of energy that shapes your collective reality. In daily life, this concept might encourage you to be more mindful of your thoughts and emotions, knowing they could influence others and the world around you.

Rupert Sheldrake's Morphic Resonance: Dr. Rupert Sheldrake proposed the theory of morphic resonance, which suggests that all natural systems, including DNA, inherit a collective memory from all previous things of their kind. This non-local information field might influence biological processes, implying that DNA could interact with a larger informational field beyond its physical structure.

Think of how quickly skills are learned over time, whether it's children picking up technology much faster than previous generations or trends spreading rapidly across cultures. Morphic resonance suggests that as more people learn or practice something, it becomes easier for others to tap into that knowledge. In daily life, this could explain why new ideas or innovations sometimes seem to "catch on" quickly across the world or why certain trends or cultural behaviors spread like wildfire. It implies that your DNA might be tapping into this collective memory, making it easier for you to learn and grow based on the experiences of others.

Water Memory and Homeopathy: The concept of water memory, though controversial, suggests that water can retain a memory of substances that were once dissolved in it, even after they have been diluted, to the point that no molecules of the original substance remain. Some researchers speculate that DNA, surrounded by water in cells, might be influenced by these informational imprints in the water, picking up and transmitting energy signals as a form of non-local interaction.

Imagine drinking water that hydrates you and contains subtle, energetic imprints that influence your health and well-being. Since your body and cells are mostly water, this might mean that the water you consume could carry information that interacts with your DNA, potentially impacting your health. Practically, it might encourage you to pay more attention to the quality of the water you drink or explore holistic practices like homeopathy, which uses the concept of energetic imprints in water to promote healing.

These examples should help you understand how these advanced concepts might apply to daily experiences, showing that your DNA could be more than just a biological blueprint—it could be a powerful receiver and transmitter of information from both local and non-local fields, impacting your awareness, health, and connection to the world around you as well as influencing consciousness and other aspects of human experience.

However, to fully grasp the deeper mechanics of DNA's role in consciousness, it's important to explore the intricate structure of DNA itself and how it operates beyond just the biological level.

The Codes of Consciousness Within DNA

Each DNA strand consists of a double helix structure, wherein one strand carries electrical properties while the other exhibits magnetic characteristics. This intricate genetic blueprint comprises 12 distinct codes, comprising 12 electrical and 12 magnetic frequency sub-codes. You can envision this complexity by likening it to a 12-inch ruler, with each inch representing a sub-frequency.

These codes function as photonic packets of information, serving as the means through which consciousness can interpret and engage with specific frequencies from various dimensions. The activation of a particular DNA strand enables consciousness not only to perceive these frequencies but also to manifest itself within your reality. Therefore, activating your DNA aims to integrate higher levels of consciousness existing within the 15 dimensional time-space matrix that encompasses your existence, allowing this consciousness to permeate and manifest in your perception of the world.

Conceptualize DNA as a "modem" that enables you to simultaneously navigate and operate within different realities, dimensions, and densities. This perspective challenges the conventional notion that DNA is solely confined to the realm of 3-D reality. In truth, DNA is multidimensional, serving as a conduit for your interaction with various planes of existence. You are not spiritually limited because you have the intrinsic ability to expand the DNA by plugging in the intron DNA particles stored in the cells, which will allow more and more of the spiritual identity to merge with the physically conscious identity. In fact, as you assemble DNA strands, perception of both past and present incarnations become progressively more available to your present conscious awareness.

Ultimately, the knowledge for your evolution and expansion is stored within your cells and your multidimensional identity. By the very intention of reaching for integration with your higher levels of identity, you automatically stimulate the dormant codes within the cells and DNA to expand. With that expansion, the multidimensional knowledge of your higher identity becomes progressively more available within the conscious awareness of the physical form. In other words, you start to remember who you truly are!

Throughout human history, we've been conditioned to see life in linear terms—birth, aging, and death, all tied to a singular physical existence. But what if this perspective is just one small facet of a much larger reality? As you begin to understand the multidimensional nature of DNA and consciousness, you open the door to a greater, more interconnected way of living that transcends the limits of time and space.

The original human blueprint was designed to be far more advanced than you experience today. This template contained 12 active strands of DNA, each holding the key to different levels of consciousness and potential. Humanity was meant to evolve by progressively activating these DNA strands, unlocking abilities beyond what we now consider normal, such as heightened intuition, the ability to transmute matter, and even immortality.

While immortality may sound like something out of mythology, ancient cultures have long told stories of beings who lived far beyond what we believe possible. These tales may not be mere fantasy. Biologist Rupert Sheldrake has explored the idea of *cellular immortality*, suggesting that cells may be able to regenerate indefinitely, hinting at the potential for human life to extend far beyond its current limits.

What prevents you from living this way now? The truth is that, due to genetic mutations and environmental distortions, humanity has been locked out of its full potential. When we are born, only three of the 12 strands of the original Blueprint are active, and the rest remain dormant, often referred to by mainstream science as 'junk DNA.' This separation and suppression of your full DNA capacity have kept you trapped in cycles of aging, disease, and death.

Our original human ancestors did not experience this limitation. They were eternal beings with bodies that did not age or die because their 12-strand DNA template was fully functional. The deterioration experienced today in what is called aging is, in fact, a result of this diminished genetic template. The energy required to sustain cellular regeneration is no longer flowing freely, leading to the gradual breakdown of the body.

The Genetic Blueprint for Youth

Recent research, like that of David Sinclair, suggests that aging is not inevitable. In his book *LifeSpan*, Sinclair explains that the genetic blueprint for youth remains intact within your DNA and gets lost due to accumulated damage over time. His work, along with studies like those by psychologist Ellen Langer, who demonstrated that simply by altering your environment and mindset, you can physiologically reverse signs of aging, highlights the potential within you to restore your original design.

Langer's study brought together eight men in their 70s and 80s to embark on a transformative five-day retreat where they were prompted to mentally transport themselves back in time - specifically, 22 years younger. Meanwhile, another group of eight elderly men, the control group, were instructed to reminisce about their past but not to mentally inhabit a younger version of themselves.

The first group experienced an immersive environment meticulously crafted to resemble the year 1959. They perused vintage issues of Life and the Saturday Evening Post, indulged in movies and television shows popular during that era, and listened to recordings of 1959 radio broadcasts. Engaging in discussions about contemporary events further anchored them in the past.

Following each five-day retreat, researchers meticulously compared physiological measurements taken before and after the study. Both groups exhibited signs of physiological rejuvenation, but the first group showed significantly greater improvement than the control group. They stood taller with improved posture, experienced greater joint flexibility, and even saw a reduction in arthritis symptoms. Their senses sharpened, cognitive abilities surged, and they displayed remarkable memory enhancement.

The most astonishing revelation was that these men appeared to reverse aging within the span of just five days physically. Some even shed their canes, partaking in activities like football. How did this remarkable transformation occur? By mentally reconnecting with their younger selves, these individuals seemingly activated neural pathways that triggered physiological changes in their bodies. The effects weren't merely psychological; they were tangible, measurable alterations in their biology.

These findings underscore the detrimental conditioning by societal beliefs regarding aging, which dictate what you can or cannot do based on your age. No doubt, at times in your life, you may have been subject to messages such as "You're too old to learn new skills," "You can't start a new career," or "It's too late to pursue your dreams." These limiting beliefs can create self-fulfilling prophecies, leading individuals to conform to these expectations and experience declining abilities and vitality. However, Dr Langer's research suggests that when you challenge these age-related stereotypes and immerse yourself in environments that encourage youthful engagement and possibilities, you can significantly enhance your well-being, proving that age is often more of a mental construct than a physical reality.

This study poses a provocative question, "are you unwittingly programmed to succumb to your biology, or do you possess the latent ability to repair and restore the youthful information in your cells and rewrite your physical destiny?"

Reclaiming Your Original Blueprint

The idea that you must age and decline is simply a program you've been conditioned to believe. Just as some can reverse aging through altered mental and environmental states, humanity has the potential to reverse the genetic mutations that limit your full potential. Imagine a life where the activation of all 12 strands of your DNA unlocks heightened sensory perception, access to higher realms of consciousness, and the ability to transcend physical limitations.

This dormant potential is waiting within you, encoded in junk DNA'—and it's far from useless. These dormant DNA strands, when activated, allow for a full connection to higher dimensions of consciousness, reconnecting you to your original purpose as an eternal being capable of extraordinary abilities.

The original blueprint was designed to help humanity evolve across multiple dimensions, moving from a dense, carbon-based biology to a more refined, light-based form. But, due to distortions in our genetic makeup, this process has been stalled. By reconnecting with this original blueprint, you can begin to heal these distortions, reactivating the higher DNA strands that will allow you to access your true potential.

The journey back to your original design is not just personal; it's a collective evolution. Everyone can heal, activate, and ascend through this process, moving from the current state of limitation toward the full realization of their multidimensional self.

As you read these words, consider the possibility that within you lies a hidden potential—a blueprint for eternal life, heightened consciousness, and the ability to transcend the physical world's limitations. The question is: will you unlock it?

Re-Imagine
YOU

An experiment conducted by Australian psychologist Alan Richardson is often cited as a compelling example of the power of mental visualization in enhancing performance, even without physical practice.

He took a group of basketball players and divided them into three groups, each with a different approach to training focused on free throws.

The first group physically practiced shooting free throws for 20 minutes every day over a set period. The second group did not engage in any physical practice; instead, they spent the same amount of time (20 minutes daily) mentally visualizing themselves successfully making free throws. The third group did not practice or visualize; they simply continued their routine without any specific training for free throws.

The results were remarkable. As expected, the players who practiced daily showed improvement in their free throw accuracy over time. However, the group that only visualized themselves making successful free throws also showed significant improvement, nearly matching the performance of those who physically practiced. The group that did not practice or visualize, predictably, showed little to no improvement.

This experiment suggests that mental rehearsal or visualization can effectively simulate physical practice. The brain doesn't always differentiate between real and imagined experiences, allowing mental exercises to reinforce neural pathways similar to actual physical training. These findings highlight the potential of visualization techniques in skill acquisition and performance enhancement across various domains, not just sports. Subsequent research in neuroscience supports Richardson's findings, showing that mental rehearsal activates the same brain regions as physical practice, leading to similar improvements in performance.

Just as Dr. Ellen Langer was able to create an environment that stimulated enormous results regarding aging and revitalization, you can do the same. Play the music you listened to twenty years ago and research what was going on in the world at that time. Spend time with friends reminiscing about the past and fully immerse yourself in that era. By recreating the atmosphere of your younger years, you can tap into the vitality and mindset of that time, potentially reversing some of the perceived effects of aging. This approach can reignite a youthful spirit, boost mental and emotional well-being, and challenge the societal norms that often limit what we believe is possible as we age. Embracing these practices can help you rediscover the energy and enthusiasm of your past, demonstrating that age is, indeed, just a number

- Create a playlist of songs that you enjoyed during your younger years. Play this music in the background to set   a nostalgic mood.

- Find TV shows, movies, or news clips from the past and spend some time watching them. Pay attention to the styles, language, and cultural references that were prevalent at the time.

- If possible, invite friends or family members who shared those years with you. Spend an hour or two reminiscing about past experiences, shared memories, and funny stories. This can be done in person or through a video call.

- Engage in activities or hobbies that you enjoyed during that period. Whether it's dancing, playing a musical instrument, or a favorite sport, spending time doing what you love can rekindle youthful energy.

- Spend 10 minutes each day in a quiet space. Close your eyes and visualize yourself in a younger body full of energy and vitality. Imagine your cells rejuvenating and your body feeling younger and stronger.

"DNA is not just the building blocks of life; it is the blueprint of our evolutionary potential, carrying within it the codes that can unlock the full spectrum of human existence."

PART TWO
SUMMARY

- Everything that will ever exist, exists in a state of potential creation. Source perpetuates itself through an eternal act of fusion and fission, like switching a light on and off. You are a Creator within creation, and taking place within in

- The physically manifest aspects of the human body represent only one small portion of the true human anatomy. Many other identities are you, and just more expanded self-realized parts of yourself. The journey is to know yourself and to become more of who you truly are.

- Due to template distortions, as soon as consciousness comes into the physical atomic body and intertwines with the DNA template, the DNA template shuts off approximately 90% of the consciousness requirements. This means you don't remember who you truly are and your true cosmic history.

- Human DNA and design are part of a greater cosmic orchestra, with origins and functions rooted in higher dimensional harmonics.

- Humans are not functioning on the original blueprint and find themselves trapped as consciousness in a mortal body form with a very short lifespan that progressively deteriorates. The physical body dies because there is not enough energy coming in to keep the perpetual motion of cellular re-genesis going.

- The process of activating your DNA is aimed at integrating higher levels of consciousness existing within the 15-dimensional time-space matrix that encompasses your existence, allowing this consciousness to permeate and manifest in your perception of the world.

Re-Imagine YOU

PART THREE

CONTAMINATED:
Hidden Hazards in Your Food & Water

From the age of 13, I found myself without an identity, reduced to a nameless label. My brother introduced me to others not as *me* but simply as "my fat little sister." I wasn't actually overweight—just carrying what my mother called "puppy fat," with the promise that it would vanish as I grew older. Except, it didn't.

Year after year, that label stuck to me like glue, a constant shadow over how I saw myself. Tired of being defined by it, I decided to take control in the only way I knew how: by drastically cutting back on food. Watching the weight fall off felt like reclaiming power over my body; a body that society had already taught me didn't fit its mold. I devised a plan: at school, I claimed to eat plenty at home, and at home, I pretended to be full of what I ate at school. In reality, I barely ate at all, surviving on salad and water, tricking my stomach into a false sense of fullness. I teetered on the edge of an eating disorder, a dangerous place that, as a vulnerable teenager, I didn't recognize.

Looking back now, I see this for what it was—conditioning—a deeply rooted web of expectations and pressures spun by society, culture, and media. From every corner, images of the "ideal" body bombarded me, whispers of what I should be and how I should look. Being slim equated to beauty, success, and self-worth. It was as if every advertisement, every movie star, every influencer was part of an invisible hand, subtly steering me toward the belief that my value hinged on how closely I matched their version of perfection.

We are raised in a world that glorifies restriction, glamorizes detoxes, and deifies "superfoods." It teaches us that thinness is a virtue and self-deprivation a strength. Society's relentless messages mold how we see food, not as nourishment but as a symbol of status, discipline, and self-worth. For many, this creates a toxic cycle of guilt, shame, bingeing, and dieting.

And it's not just society. Our upbringing, too, quietly shapes our relationship with food. Think about it: was food used as a reward or punishment in your childhood? Were you taught to clear your plate, no matter how full you were? These early experiences leave lasting marks. For some, food becomes a crutch, a source of comfort when life feels overwhelming. For others, it becomes something to control, to restrict, as a way of asserting dominance over emotions, over the world.

I'm fortunate that my unhealthy relationship with food didn't last long. By my late teens, I had broken free, choosing instead to nourish myself in a way that aligned with my inner truth. Becoming vegetarian wasn't just a dietary choice—it was a declaration of autonomy over my body and my health, a way to step out of the societal noise and listen to my own intuition. It led me toward a lighter, more mindful way of eating, and for that, I'm grateful.

However, the truth is the conditioning around food and body image is pervasive. For so many, food becomes a battleground where self-worth, acceptance, and identity are fought over with every meal. And yet, it doesn't have to be this way. Imagine a world where nourishment is seen not as a weapon or a reward but as the act of love, which is meant to be fuel for your mind, body, and spirit.

In this section, I challenge you to unearth the conditioning that has shaped your relationship with food. Question everything you've been told about what it means to nourish yourself. Do you eat to conform to society's expectations, or do you eat to thrive? Are you living for you or for the version of you that the world tells you to be?

This is an invitation to break free from the chains of cultural and societal programming and open your mind to alternative ways of sustaining yourself and in ways that foster health, mindfulness, and freedom. You have the power to reclaim your body, not as something to be molded to fit someone else's ideals, but as the vibrant, powerful vessel it was always meant to be.

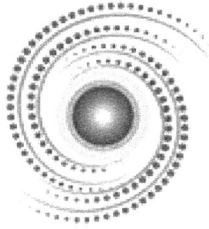

Chapter Five
Bioregenesis of the
Human DNA Blueprint

What if everything you've been told about your body, about its limits, it's inevitable aging, and its ultimate demise, was only a fraction of the truth? What if your cells, your DNA, and your very essence hold secrets far beyond the understanding of mainstream science? What if you possessed the power to unlock these secrets and, in doing so, reclaim abilities thought to belong only to ancient myths or science fiction?

The Sleeping Giant Within

The reality is that only a rare few truly grasp the astonishing capabilities encoded within their bodies. For too long, you've been led to believe that your physical form is who you are and that when your body dies, your existence simply ends. But what if that's just the surface of the story? Deep within your cells lies an astonishing potential—a memory of your origins that stretches far beyond the boundaries of Earth, waiting for you to tap into it. Hidden in your DNA are the codes for transcendence, for healing, and for a life of unimaginable vitality.

Bioregenesis is not just a buzzword. It's the key to unlocking these dormant capabilities. Imagine a life where the physical, mental, and emotional constraints of the human experience could be rewired, allowing you to bypass aging, disease, and degeneration. This is not just a hypothetical dream; it's a path you can walk today.

Biohacking & Bioregenesis: The Revolution Has Already Begun

In recent years, a movement has been gaining momentum: biohacking. It's a trend that's caught the attention of everyone from Silicon Valley executives to wellness enthusiasts, all seeking to optimize their bodies and minds in ways previously thought impossible. Biohackers are rewriting the rulebook on what it means to be human. They use science, technology, and ancient wisdom to hack their biology and improve cognitive function, extend their lifespan, and even enhance their physical capabilities.

From intravenous (IV) nutrient therapy to brain-enhancing supplements, biohackers are pushing the boundaries of what the body can achieve. Nutritional supplements, fasting, and specific diets all play a crucial role in biohacking. By optimizing the body's biological processes, biohackers aim to achieve optimal health and improve physical and mental performance. But what if these modern techniques were only scratching the surface? What if bioregenesis and the idea that the human body can not only heal itself but rebuild itself held the key to something much more profound?

The Memory of Immortality: Is It Still Locked Inside Us?

Imagine for a moment that every cell in your body holds the memory of perfect health. This isn't just some far-fetched sci-fi fantasy. Leading scientists and researchers like David Sinclair and Candace Pert have already shown that the blueprint for cellular regeneration is embedded in your DNA. Every time your cells divide, they're passing along not just your genetic material but also the instructions for how to exist in perfect harmony with your environment and how to thrive. Sadly, over time, this memory has become distorted, buried beneath layers of genetic mutations and environmental toxins.

The truth is your body was once designed for eternal life. The concept of death, aging, and disease? These are deviations from the original design. The real question is not whether you *can* heal but whether you can reclaim the full potential encoded within you.

Bioregenesis doesn't just focus on healing the physical body. It recognizes the intricate dance between emotions, consciousness, and biology. Chronic stress, depression, and emotional trauma aren't just states of mind; they're energy patterns that can warp the very fabric of your DNA. Can you reverse the damage? Can you change the trajectory of your health? Absolutely, if you understand how to realign your emotional and physical selves.

Consider the power of your own beliefs. Numerous studies have shown the incredible effects of the placebo, where just believing something will heal you can trigger profound physiological changes. From pain relief in post-surgery patients to chronic conditions vanishing, the placebo effect demonstrates the raw power of the mind-body connection.

What if this wasn't a placebo at all? What if the sheer act of intention and of truly believing in your ability to regenerate—could spark real, tangible changes at the cellular level? Bioregenesis isn't just a practice; it's a revolution in how we perceive health and healing.

Source Feeding: The Ultimate DNA Reboot

Just suppose you could bypass food entirely and rely on pure energy to fuel your body, mind, and spirit? The idea of living without eating, more commonly known as breatharianism, Source feeding, or pranic living, is one of the most controversial yet fascinating areas of exploration. This is not about starvation. It's about tapping into the energy of the universe itself, a practice that has been whispered about for centuries, only now resurfacing in modern discourse. By shifting from external food sources to direct energetic sustenance, you can begin to heal and reactivate your dormant DNA, reclaiming the full potential of the human body.

This practice, once the domain of mystics and sages, is slowly making its way back into the mainstream, raising questions about our relationship with food, nourishment, and even the very nature of energy itself. Could it be that our dependency on food is part of the same genetic distortion that has trapped us in the cycles of birth, aging, and death?

You've been conditioned to believe that aging and death are inevitable. That diseases are random, that healing takes time—or worse, that it's impossible. But what if those beliefs were the real prison? What if, by shifting your consciousness, energy, and perception, you could literally rewrite the script of your own DNA, bringing it back to its original, untainted form?

Junk DNA: The Hidden Treasure of Human Potential

The concept of *junk DNA* - the 97% of your genetic material that remains a mystery to modern science - holds the key. This "junk" isn't junk at all. It's the dormant code of your full potential, waiting for you to switch it on. And once it's activated, who knows what you might become?

Imagine a grand, ancient library hidden and known to only a few. This library is filled with countless books, scrolls, and manuscripts, some of which are centuries old. The library has two main sections: the well-lit area where visitors come and read the well-known books and a vast, dimly lit section where many books are covered in dust, their contents unknown and unread for generations.

For years, people believed that the books in the well-lit area contained all the knowledge the library had to offer. They referred to the dimly lit section as the "junk room," thinking it was unimportant. But one day, a curious scholar explored this neglected library part.

As the scholars dusted off the first book, they discovered ancient texts filled with wisdom and knowledge lost to time. These texts contained advanced insights about the universe, secrets to enhancing human potential and forgotten histories. Excited, the scholar began to share these findings with the world.

It turned out that the so-called "junk room" was actually a treasure trove of untapped knowledge and potential. The more people explored, the more they realized that these forgotten books were essential to understanding the complete picture of their history, culture, and capabilities. They found solutions to problems they thought unsolvable, new technologies, and a deeper understanding of their own existence.

Similarly, your DNA has sections that scientists label as "junk" because they have yet to understand its purpose. Recent research reveals that this non-coding DNA, much like the forgotten books in the library, holds immense potential and critical information. These DNA segments play roles in regulating gene expression, maintaining the integrity of your chromosomes, and possibly even influencing your development and evolution.

Just as the scholar uncovered the hidden value of the neglected books, scientists are now discovering that "junk" DNA is far from useless. It is a vital part of our genetic library, filled with possibilities waiting to be explored and understood.

These segments of DNA, seemingly inactive and unproductive in protein synthesis, were once repositories of life's fundamental components. As you delve deeper, you begin to comprehend their pivotal role in your existence, even opening to the possibility that further chromosomes and nucleotides could be discovered to assist in your expansion.

Reclaiming Your Original DNA Potential

Bioregenesis of the human DNA blueprint refers to restoring your original potential, even in the face of DNA degradation. Despite the damage inflicted upon our genetic structure through cosmic conflicts that have spanned eons, there remains a possibility to initiate healing and reclaim the atomic integrity that was once lost.

This potential for renewal is rooted in the universe and cosmos, both crafted by Source with the gift of free will. In your individualized state, you are given a choice: you can align with Source and adhere to the natural laws of creation, thus perpetuating eternal life and continuous creation, or you can choose to deviate from this path.

When power is mismanaged, it often leads to a cyclical existence—much like a hamster running endlessly on a wheel. In this state, you may find yourself living life after life without the possibility of true freedom. This endless cycle is not a product of Source but rather the result of a consciousness that has chosen to explore divergent expressions. Such explorations have led to finite resources and limited lifespans, distancing humanity from its connection to a broader cosmic reality. This disconnection has caused a depletion of the vital energy needed to sustain the natural process of cellular regenesis, leading to the eventual demise of the physical body.

Free will is a powerful gift, allowing you to make choices that either support the manifestation of desired outcomes in harmony with Universal Laws or oppose these laws, resulting in finite life, resource scarcity, competition, and the survival of the fittest. The path you choose shapes the reality you experience.

Re-Imagine
YOU

I grew up immersed in a world of alternative health and healing interventions, thanks to my extraordinary mother, who introduced me to the principles of homeopathy and Bach Flower Remedies from an early age. Though different in their methodologies, these approaches to health share a common belief in the body's innate ability to heal itself when supported by natural, gentle remedies.

Homeopathy is based on the principle of "like cures," where substances that produce symptoms in a healthy person can, in extremely diluted forms, treat similar symptoms in someone who is ill. The idea is that these highly diluted substances trigger the body's natural defenses, promoting healing by encouraging the body to respond to the illness energetically. My mother often used homeopathic remedies to address a wide range of issues, from common colds to more chronic conditions, trusting in the subtle yet profound effects these remedies could have on our overall well-being.

On the other hand, Bach Flower Remedies focus on emotional and mental well-being, believing that imbalances in these areas can manifest as physical illness. Dr. Edward Bach, the creator of these remedies, identified 38 different flowers, each associated with a specific emotional state. By using these flower essences, the goal is to restore emotional harmony, which in turn supports physical health. My mother often turned to Bach Flower Remedies to help us navigate emotional challenges, using them as a tool to bring balance and peace during times of stress or upheaval.

Growing up with these alternative practices instilled in me a deep respect for the body's natural healing processes and a belief in the power of gentle, non-invasive treatments. My mother's dedication to these methods was not just about treating illness but about fostering a holistic approach to health that considered the emotional, mental, and physical aspects of well-being. This upbringing has profoundly shaped my understanding of health and healing, grounding me in believing that true wellness comes from supporting the body's innate wisdom with care and compassion.

Here are some powerful questions designed to help uncover your beliefs, programming, and conditioning around eating, health, and healing:

Programming Around Health:

- o What were the messages you received about health growing up?

- o How do you define health, and where do those definitions come from?

- o Do you believe that health is something within your control? Why or why not?

- o What are your thoughts on the connection between mind, body, and health?

- o How do you react to the idea of healing without conventional medicine?

- o What habits or routines do you believe are essential for maintaining health?

- o How do you feel about your body's ability to heal itself?

Conditioning Around Healing:

- o What do you believe is necessary for healing to take place?

- o How do you view the role of emotions and thoughts in the healing process?

- o Does healing require external interventions, or can it come from within?

- o How do you feel about alternative healing practices? What has shaped those feelings?

o   What do you believe about the body's natural state – is it one of health, imbalance, or something else?

o   How do you respond to illness or physical discomfort? What do you think that response says about your beliefs?

o   What stories have you been told about healing and recovery, and how have they impacted you?

These questions are designed to provoke deep reflection, encouraging an exploration of the underlying beliefs and conditioning that shape your approach to eating, health, and healing.

"The body possesses an extraordinary capacity to repair and heal itself, and when supported correctly, it can unlock profound regenerative potential, restoring balance and vitality at the deepest levels."

Re-Imagine **YOU**

Chapter Six

Toxic Consumption:
Unveiling the Risks in Your Food

KEY QUESTIONS:

Nourishment or Neglect?
Do you know what is in your food and water?
Are you ready to explore alternative nourishment?

The concept of food as more than just sustenance taps into the profound relationship between what you eat and who you are. While solid food is commonly viewed as the body's fuel, providing the essential nutrients and energy needed for survival, its role extends far beyond mere physical nourishment. Food is deeply woven into the fabric of culture, tradition, and personal identity, influencing your habits, choices, and even emotional responses.

How Food Shapes Identity and Emotion

From a young age, food is associated with a variety of experiences that shape your relationship with it. For example, food often plays a central role in cultural traditions and customs. Think of the special meals prepared during holidays, religious ceremonies, or family gatherings— these meals are not just about eating but about connection, celebration, and continuity. The specific foods you eat during these occasions often carry symbolic meanings, are passed down through generations, and are tied to your sense of identity and belonging.

In addition, food has historically been used as a tool for behavior management. Many people grow up associating food with reward or punishment - being given a treat for good behavior or having dessert withheld as a consequence. This early conditioning can create deep-seated associations between food and emotions, leading to habits that persist into adulthood, such as using food for comfort during stressful times or feeling guilty after indulging in something deemed "unhealthy."

The sensory experience of food also plays a powerful role in shaping your responses to it. For instance, the sound of an ice cream van or the smell of freshly baked bread can evoke strong, almost automatic reactions. These responses are deeply conditioned and rooted in the pleasure or comfort these foods have provided. The mere anticipation of these foods can trigger cravings, emotional responses, or even memories, underscoring the profound connection between food, senses, and emotions.

Given this intricate relationship with food, shifting to an alternative source of nourishment- such as exploring practices like fasting, liquid diets, or even more esoteric approaches like Source feeding (breatharianism) can challenge deeply ingrained habits, traditions, beliefs, mindsets, and emotions. Such a shift can bring up resistance, as it often requires confronting and dismantling long-held patterns that are deeply embedded in both the psyche and the body's cellular memory.

For instance, the act of eating is often linked to comfort, security, and love. Changing this dynamic might initially feel unsettling, as it challenges the unconscious associations built over a lifetime. It can also prompt reevaluating how you connect with culture, family, and self-identity, as food is often a cornerstone of these connections.

Moreover, there is an emerging understanding in fields like epigenetics that your relationship with food can influence your DNA and gene expression. This means that the habits, choices, and emotional states associated with eating can have a biological impact, potentially reinforcing or altering patterns passed down through generations.

Shifting to alternative forms of nourishment requires not just a change in diet but a profound exploration of the deeply rooted habits, mindsets, and emotions that have been shaped by a lifetime of eating and the cultural and familial contexts in which it occurs.

Energy Over Matter: The Shift from Food to Prana

In a 1901 article entitled Talking With The Planets, famed inventor Nikola Tesla wrote, "Why should a living being not be able to obtain all the energy it needs for the performance of its life functions from the environment, instead of through the consumption of food, and transforming, by a complicated process, the energy of chemical combinations into life-sustaining energy?"

Tesla's revolutionary idea speaks to a deeper truth - perhaps the true hunger we feel isn't for physical sustenance but something far more profound. In your quest for fulfillment, do you harbor a longing that transcends the mundane aspects of existence? Whether love, spirituality, success, or another deeply sought-after aspiration, you may find yourself overindulging, not in the nourishment of the soul, but in material comforts. Feasting excessively on food and drink, you might attempt to satisfy the hunger within, unaware that these physical indulgences merely mask the deeper cravings of your being.

Instead of tuning in to your body to assess if you're really hungry, many fall into the habit of eating according to the time of day. In other words, rather than questioning whether nourishment is genuinely needed, you may be governed by the clock. It's breakfast time, you need to eat. It's lunchtime, and time for another meal. And so it goes, with snacks in between, and you eat simply because of the hour on the clock rather than any true physiological need, and while your body may be overfed, the spirit remains famished. In the quest for contentment, perhaps it's time to redirect your focus inward, nourishing the self with the sustenance you crave to find genuine fulfillment beyond the superficial pleasures of excess.

Obesity: When Excess Turns Against You

As a result of this feasting obsession, obesity is now a widespread issue plaguing societies across the globe. Stemming from a combination of genetic, environmental, behavioral, and socio-economic factors, the health implications of obesity are profound, increasing the risk of various chronic conditions such as type 2 diabetes, cardiovascular disease, certain cancers, and musculoskeletal disorders.

Obesity has profound effects on DNA, contributing to genetic alterations and epigenetic modifications that impact cellular function and overall health. Studies have shown that obesity is associated with increased oxidative stress, inflammation, and insulin resistance, all of which can damage DNA. This damage can manifest in various forms, including DNA strand breaks, chromosomal abnormalities, and alterations in DNA methylation patterns.

Are We Gorging Ourselves to Death? Dr. Shatalova's Bold Claim

"Are We Really Gorging Ourselves to Death" is a controversial book written by Russian physician Dr. Galina Shatalova. Not only does she believe that we are gorging ourselves to death, but she also proposes that the body is designed to live vitally for at least 150 years. Shatalova insists that a healthy human body is designed to process live plant foods and does not need more than 250 - 400 calories to maintain its basic metabolic needs. Foods eaten beyond those low basic needs burden a healthy system with additional eliminatory tasks, consequently shortening the human lifespan.

This forward-thinking physician challenges people to reconsider the common theory of balanced nutrition and questions if food is the only source with which humans can provide for their energy needs. From a logical perspective, Dr. Galina is sure you will find that you are immersed in energy from solar energy, ocean water, and the energy of the physical vacuum around you.

Shatalova also claims that people need less than a tenth of the water we are told to take in under stressful situations. To prove her point, she invited a group of athletes to participate in a seven-day super-marathon of 500 kilometers, at 70-72 km per day, and with the restricted caloric and water intake she advocates. This kind of demand on the human system is considered extremely stressful, with more than the stress of an average marathon.

In keeping with the ideas of balanced nutrition, the athletes had meals consisting of 190 grams of protein, 2000 grams of fat, and 900 grams of carbohydrates, all adding up to a whopping 6000 calories!

The athletes of Shatalovas' own group took in just 28 grams of protein, 25 grams of fat, and 180 grams of carbohydrates, which added up to 1200 calories made up of fresh vegetables and fruits in whole form rather than juice and whole grains. In the final analysis, her athletes were much less compromised from the stress and more vital at the end of the race than their carb-loaded colleagues. And amazingly, they did not lose any weight.

While the role of calorie restriction in humans is controversial, new data in monkeys and humans have provided new insights into the potential role of calorie restriction in longevity.

Have you been lied to regarding what is really required to nourish and sustain yourself?

In recent years, several documentaries have shed light on the poor quality of food and its impact on health, society, and the environment. Here are some notable ones:

1. **Food, Inc. (2008)**: Directed by Robert Kenner, this documentary examines the industrialization of the food system in the United States, highlighting issues such as factory farming, the use of pesticides and genetically modified organisms (GMOs), and the influence of corporate interests on food production.

2. **Fed Up (2014)**: Narrated by Katie Couric, this documentary explores the causes and consequences of the obesity epidemic in

the United States, focusing on the role of the food industry, government policies, and marketing tactics in promoting unhealthy diets high in sugar and processed foods.

3. **What the Health (2017)**: Directed by Kip Andersen and Keegan Kuhn, this documentary investigates the link between diet and chronic diseases such as heart disease, diabetes, and cancer. It explores the influence of the pharmaceutical and food industries on public health policies and advocates for a plant-based diet.

4. **The Magic Pill (2017)**: This documentary follows individuals with chronic health conditions as they adopt a ketogenic diet, high in fats and low in carbohydrates. It explores the potential benefits of this diet for improving health outcomes and challenges conventional dietary recommendations.

5. **Forks Over Knives (2011)**: Directed by Lee Fulkerson, this documentary examines the scientific evidence supporting a whole-food, plant-based diet to prevent and reverse chronic diseases. It interviews medical experts and follows individuals who have adopted this dietary approach.

6. **Rotten (2018)**: This Netflix documentary series explores various aspects of the global food industry, including corruption in the honey industry, the impact of food allergies on the supply chain, and the challenges faced by farmers and fishermen.

7. **Super-Size Me (2004)**: Directed by Morgan Spurlock, this documentary follows Spurlock as he consumes only McDonald's food for 30 days to explore the health effects of a fast-food diet. It highlights the prevalence of obesity and related health issues in the United States.

In a world where the quality of food, water, and air is rapidly deteriorating, the path to becoming Source-fed is no longer just an esoteric concept; it is an urgent and revolutionary solution for safeguarding your health and unlocking your true potential. With every meal, every breath of polluted air, and every sip of contaminated water, you are ingesting toxins and damaging your DNA, inhibiting your ability to access higher sensory perception and thrive in alignment with your innate capabilities.

Transitioning to this lifestyle, where nourishment is drawn from prana's pure, boundless energy, presents a radical yet increasingly viable alternative for those seeking to free themselves from the poisons of modern living. By embracing Source feeding, you are choosing to regenerate your body at the deepest level, protect your DNA, and activate a state of heightened awareness, free from the environmental pollutants that steadily compromise human potential. Let's explore why making this shift is not just a possibility but a powerful step toward reclaiming your health and vitality in an increasingly toxic world.

The Hazards Lurking in Our Food: Unveiling DNA Damage Caused by Food Additives

Welcome to the modern era of food convenience, where the seductive lure of flavor-enhancing additives and quick fixes dominates diets. But beneath the surface of artificial colors and preservatives, beneath every bite of processed food, lies a hidden truth: your DNA is under siege. What may seem like a harmless indulgence is, in fact, a direct assault on your genetic blueprint, slowly unraveling the very essence of your health.

Scientific evidence is uncovering a chilling reality: many common food additives are silently wreaking havoc on your DNA, setting the stage for genetic mutations and chronic disease. Take synthetic food colorings, for example—the vibrant hues that make your food pop are doing the same to your DNA, with their genotoxic properties causing actual damage to your genetic material. Every time you consume them, you risk triggering dangerous mutations that could lead to irreversible health issues.

Then, there are preservatives like sodium nitrite and sodium nitrate commonly found in processed meats. These aren't just extending shelf life—they're actively promoting DNA damage, forming carcinogenic compounds in your body that increase your risk of cancer and other diseases. You're not just eating a sandwich; you're consuming a ticking time bomb of oxidative stress and genetic degradation.

Let's not forget the horror show of "fake food" from China, where counterfeit products like plastic rice, synthetic eggs, and tainted seafood flood markets packed with toxins and devoid of real nutrition. Every bite of these fraudulent foods is an assault on your health, leaving your body fighting against the very substances meant to sustain it.

Even your favorite fast foods aren't innocent. The high temperatures in cooking red meat and vegetables silently degrade your DNA. Studies link this cooking process to cancer, cardiovascular disease, and a shorter lifespan. Each charred burger or crispy vegetable may taste delicious, but behind the scenes, it's chipping away at the very foundation of your health.

And what about those "zero-calorie" artificial sweeteners? Aspartame, often marketed as a healthier choice, has been shown to disrupt the regulation of your genes, potentially leading to metabolic disorders like obesity and diabetes. It's a sugar-free trap that's distorting your genetic code while promising guilt-free indulgence.

Then there's the ever-present threat of pesticides. Designed to kill pests, these toxic chemicals are also wreaking havoc on your DNA. Every fruit, vegetable, or grain grown with pesticides carries a hidden danger— studies show that pesticide exposure causes DNA strand breaks and oxidative damage, laying the groundwork for long-term health consequences.

What's even more alarming is that it's not just individual ingredients doing the damage—it's the cumulative effect. Every processed meal, pesticide-laden vegetable, and artificial sweetener contributes to a perfect storm, amplifying the destruction of your DNA with every bite. Your body is constantly battling a cocktail of toxins that distort, mutate, and damage your DNA, setting the stage for diseases like cancer.

In essence, your food isn't just fueling your body; it's rewriting your DNA. And if that doesn't shock you, it should. Every meal is a choice between nourishing your genetic potential or accelerating your DNA's destruction. The stakes have never been higher.

The Genetic Perils Lurking in Our Drinking Water: DNA Damage from Contaminants

Water, a vital resource, the very substance you depend on for your life, is no longer the pure elixir it once was. Every sip you take may deliver more than just hydration; it could silently sabotage your DNA. In a world where water sources are increasingly tainted, the consequences on your health could be far more dire than you've been led to believe.

Let's start with heavy metals. Arsenic, for example, a naturally occurring contaminant found in many water supplies, isn't just toxic; it's a DNA assassin. Long-term exposure to arsenic-laden water can wreak havoc on your genetic code, leading to mutations that increase the risk of cancers, including skin, lung, and bladder cancers. And arsenic isn't alone in its assault on your DNA.

Lead, another insidious contaminant often leaching from aging pipes, is notorious for its toxic effects. Lead exposure doesn't just mess with your mind, it attacks your genes. It damages DNA, alters gene expression, and disrupts the critical functions of your cells. For infants and children, the impact is even more devastating, causing irreversible cognitive damage and developmental delays.

But it doesn't stop there. Modern water is becoming a cocktail of emerging contaminants, from the chemicals in non-stick cookware to those used in waterproof products. These substances have been linked to DNA damage, immune system breakdowns, and reproductive disorders. Even bottled water, the supposed "safe" alternative, is contaminated with microplastics - tiny toxic particles that have been found to accumulate harmful chemicals capable of disrupting your DNA and cellular health. Meanwhile, agricultural runoff and industrial waste dump a host of pollutants into our water systems, including pesticides, pharmaceuticals, and endocrine disruptors. These toxins are linked to DNA damage and push human health to its breaking point.

And if that wasn't enough, the very water of this planet is energetically "dead." Due to distortions in the Earth's energy grids and the misalignment of human DNA, the water you drink no longer promotes longevity. It may keep you alive, but it's not keeping you well.

Now let's dive into something even more shocking: deuterium, the "heavy hydrogen" isotope lurking in your water. Unlike the lighter hydrogen you're familiar with, deuterium carries extra weight—literally. With a proton and a neutron in its nucleus, deuterium has a mass that poses serious health risks. Although it exists in small amounts (around 150 parts per million), this heavy hydrogen is no trivial matter. Scientific studies show that elevated deuterium levels interfere with your body's ability to repair DNA, potentially causing mutations that lead to long-term health problems.

Think about that: the water you drink daily could actively sabotage your genetic code. Higher deuterium levels have been linked to compromised DNA repair mechanisms, slowing down your body's ability to heal and regenerate. The good news? There's a growing awareness of this threat, and you can actually seek out Deuterium-Depleted Water specially designed to minimize this genetic burden.

So, next time you take a sip of water, ask yourself: Are you hydrating your body or slowly eroding your DNA? The choices you make today could be the key to protecting your genetic future.

Supplement Safety and Hidden Parasitic Risks

In an age marked by convenience and rapid industrialization, it is easy to understand that the nutritional value of your food and water is being reduced at an alarming rate. What is the consequence? There is a growing dependency on supplements to bridge the gap between what is consumed and what your body truly needs. Sadly, much of what is consumed in the name of supplements might as well be flushed down the drain.

The foundation of the food chain lies in the soil, yet modern agricultural practices have ravaged its nutritional integrity. Industrial farming techniques prioritize yield and profit over soil health, leading to the widespread depletion of essential nutrients. According to a study published in the Journal of the American College of Nutrition, the levels of essential minerals like calcium, iron, and magnesium have decreased by up to 40% in some cases.

Faced with the reality of nutrition-depleted food and water, in response, the global supplement industry has exploded into a lucrative industry offering an expanding array of pills, powders, and potions promising health and vitality. From multivitamins to herbal extracts, the market is flooded with products claiming to fill the nutritional gaps the modern diet leaves.

However, a staggering number of supplements on the market are of dubious quality. In fact, an investigation by the New York State Attorney General's office in 2015 found that many popular supplements contained cheap fillers and unlisted ingredients, raising serious concerns about their safety. The efficacy of supplements themselves is a subject of debate among experts, with little to no evidence of their effectiveness.

There is yet another silent predator to consider that poses a serious threat to health and well-being.

Parasites are organisms that thrive by feeding off other living beings, including humans. They come in various forms, from microscopic protozoa to larger worms, and can enter your body through contaminated food, water, or soil. Once inside, they can wreak havoc on your digestive, immune, and overall health.

Parasitic infections often go undetected for extended periods, masquerading as vague symptoms or mimicking other common ailments. However, their presence can lead to a host of serious health issues, including chronic fatigue, digestive disorders, nutrient deficiencies, and even neurological problems.

Parasites are remarkably skilled at evading the body's natural defenses, making their eradication a complex challenge that often requires targeted interventions. These invaders can linger for years, quietly draining your vitality and undermining your resilience when left unchecked.

Despite the significant diseases they can cause, parasite cleansing is an often overlooked aspect of modern healthcare. This neglect becomes even more concerning in the context of growing awareness about the harmful effects of our current sources of nourishment.

In light of these concerns, exploring Source feeding emerges as a compelling alternative. This approach offers a path to improved health and healing and holds the potential to repair DNA damage and allow you to access higher sensory perception. By reducing reliance on conventional nourishment like food and water, you can minimize pollution exposure while tapping into alternative energy sources.

Embracing this shift in nourishment opens new possibilities for health, healing, and the expansion of human potential.

Re-Imagine
YOU

Food Diary Exercise: Awakening to Your Eating Habits

This exercise is designed to help you become more aware of your eating habits, motivations, and the impact of your food and drink choices on your emotions, energy levels, and overall well-being. By tracking your eating patterns for 7-10 days, you'll gain insights into why you eat, how your body responds, and how your choices align with your true needs.

For the next 7-10 days, keep a detailed record of everything you eat and drink, along with the following observations for each meal or snack:

1. **Time:**
   Note the time you ate or drank something.

2. **Why You Ate:**
   Reflect on the reason for eating. Were you:
   o Bored?
   o Depressed?
   o Happy?
   o Socializing?
   o Eating because it was time?
   o Truly hungry?
   o Other reasons?

3. **Emotions and Feelings:**
   o **Before Eating:**
     How were you feeling right before you decided to eat? (e.g., anxious, excited, neutral)
   o **During Eating:**
     How did you feel while eating? (e.g., satisfied, guilty, relaxed)

o   **After Eating:**
How did you feel immediately after finishing? (e.g., energized, sluggish, content)

4. **Energy Levels:**
    o   **Before Eating:**
Were you feeling energetic, tired, or somewhere in between?
    o   **After Eating:**
Did your energy increase, decrease, or stay the same?

5. **Social Context:**
    o   **Who Were You With?**
Were you eating alone, with family, friends, colleagues, or others?

6. **Food & Drink Choices:**
    o   Write down exactly what you ate and drank, including portion sizes, if possible.

Reflection Questions

After completing the diary, take some time to reflect on your findings:

- Do you notice any patterns in why you eat? Are there specific emotions or situations that trigger eating?
- How does your food and drink intake affect your energy levels? Are there certain foods that consistently make you feel better or worse?
- How does the presence of others influence your eating habits? Do you tend to eat more, less, or differently when you're with certain people?
- Has this exercise changed the way you view your eating habits? Are there any areas where you feel you could make more conscious choices?

This exercise serves as a wake-up call to our often-unconscious choices around food and drink. By bringing awareness to your habits, emotions, and energy levels, you can make more intentional decisions supporting your well-being and aligning with your true needs.

"Do you eat to live, nourishing your body with intention, or live to eat, letting food dictate your life? The choice shapes your well-being and purpose."

PART THREE
SUMMARY

- Bioregenesis is a new practice based on the understanding that the human body can repair and regenerate itself.

- So-called "junk" DNA is far from useless. It is a vital part of your genetic library, filled with possibilities to be explored and understood.

- According to Dr Shatalova, a healthy human body is designed to process live plant foods and does not need more than 250 - 400 calories to maintain its basic metabolic needs.

- The accumulation of contaminants in food, water, and air poses significant risks to your health, including further damage to your DNA, which means you cannot access higher sensory perception and actualize your full potential.

- Parasites are organisms that thrive by feeding off other living beings, including humans. Once inside, they can wreak havoc on your digestive, immune, and overall health.

- Your cells do not directly absorb the nutrients from the food you consume. Instead, the body has a sophisticated system in place to break down the food into smaller components that can be utilized by the cells.

Dr. Carol Talbot

Re-Imagine **YOU**

Reimagining Nourishment:
Harnessing the Energy of Life

Over a decade ago, I found myself soaring above the dense, untouched wilderness of the Ecuadorian rainforest, a vast green sea of life spreading endlessly below. In a small 5-seater plane, I was heading deeper into the Earth's lungs, the heart of a living, breathing ecosystem far removed from the modern world. As we descended, the sheer immensity of this ancient land hit me like a wave. This was not just a forest; it was a thriving, pulsing entity, alive with a force I had never before felt so acutely. Tears welled up in my eyes, not from sadness but from a deep, unexplainable connection to something far greater than myself. This primal, nourishing energy coursed through every living thing here, including me.

At that moment, I was more than a traveler. I was part of a living, energetic web—an intricate dance of life, fueled not by food but by the raw, vibrant energy of existence itself. The air, thick with humidity, carried a vitality that seemed to breathe life into every cell of my body. The colors, the sounds of wildlife, the pulse of the earth beneath my feet all felt as if the rainforest itself was feeding me, not with food, but with pure, unfiltered life force. I felt energized, alive, and profoundly nourished in ways that transcended the physical.

What I experienced was more than an emotional or physical reaction. It was a direct interaction with the life-sustaining energy all around me. We often overlook or dismiss this deeper, energetic nourishment in our modern world, but it is always there, quietly flowing through every aspect of our lives. We have become numb to it, distracted by convenience and consumption, but imagine this: every color you see is energy, oscillating at specific frequencies, nourishing your senses. Every sound you hear is a wave of energy, vibrating in harmony with your mind and body. Even your thoughts and emotions are energetic forces capable of uplifting or depleting you.

Have you ever walked into a room and felt a palpable shift in energy, an unspoken vibe that makes you feel either invigorated or uneasy? These sensations aren't just psychological; they are the result of your innate sensitivity to the subtle energies that constantly surround you. You are, at your core, an energy-sensitive being, interacting with the world on levels you may not even realize.

In this section, I invite you to embark on a journey of reimagining nourishment, not just from food but from the energy that permeates every aspect of your life. Imagine being nourished by the pure essence of prana, the life force that flows through all living things. By tuning in to the vibrational energy of your environment, of colors, of sounds, and even your own thoughts, you can unlock an endless reservoir of vitality. This is a path toward becoming more attuned to the world's subtle energies, allowing you to sustain and energize yourself in ways that go beyond the limitations of physical sustenance.

This is not just a change in how you eat; it's a shift in how you live and how you connect with the life force that constantly surrounds you. It's an awakening to a new way of being nourished and one that taps into the boundless energy of the universe itself.

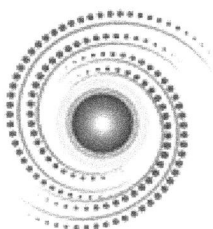

Chapter Seven
Beyond the Physical:
Energy Nourishment through Pranic Practices

KEY QUESTIONS:

What elevates your energy?
What depletes your energy?
How do you truly feed and nourish your cells?

Do you remember the story of the wicked witch in *Snow White*? Each day, she gazed into her enchanted mirror, asking, "Mirror, mirror on the wall, who is the fairest of them all?" Obsessed with the idea of beauty and youth, she desperately sought validation from a reflection that could only show her the surface—a superficial image that she believed defined her worth.

Isn't this how many of us approach our own lives? We look into metaphorical mirrors every day, seeking external validation, chasing fleeting markers of youth like wrinkle-free skin, perfect hair, or the latest diet fad. But what if, like the witch, we've been asking the wrong question all along? What if instead of asking who is the fairest, we wondered: *What nourishes the energy that sustains me?*

The witch's tragic flaw was her inability to look beyond the physical, to recognize that true beauty and true vitality come not from appearances but from the energy within. She sought eternal youth through external means, just as we often turn to cosmetic fixes or diets without addressing the deeper layers of our energy and consciousness.

This obsession with maintaining a youthful facade often overlooks the broader, more holistic approaches to vitality and longevity. From an early age, we're taught to accept that certain signs, such as greying hair or wrinkles, are inevitable as we grow older. However, have you ever stopped to ask yourself: *Is it just the passing of time that ages me, or could it be something deeper?*

The Illusion of Youth: Chasing Longevity in All the Wrong Places

Have you considered that the food and beverages you consume might be contributing to premature aging? While modern interventions like Botox and fillers offer temporary solutions, there are cultures—like those in the famed "Blue Zones"—that have embraced more sustainable, energy-driven approaches to longevity for centuries.

The residents of Okinawa, for instance, enjoy one of the highest life expectancies on the planet. Their secret lies not only in their diet of vegetables, tofu, and seaweed but also in their approach to eating mindfully, stopping at 80% fullness—a practice known as *Hara Hachi Bu*. It's not just what they eat but how they live, integrating nourishment with community, movement, and purpose.

But even these practices only skim the surface of a deeper truth: vitality and longevity stem from something beyond the physical. True energy and nourishment begin at an energetic level long before the food we eat reaches our cells.

Energy is Eternal: The Transformation of Life Force

It's often forgotten that at the core of our existence, we are energy. The human body is a dynamic interplay of energy fields, and energy, according to the laws of thermodynamics, cannot be destroyed; it can only be transformed. What if aging, decay, and the breakdown of our physical bodies are simply expressions of energy in flux, changing from one state to another?

Consider that the body, at its most fundamental level, is composed of cells powered by energy conversion processes. Cellular respiration, metabolism, and even thought patterns are energetic events that shape our health and vitality. When energy flows freely and is transformed harmoniously, the body thrives. When energy is blocked or depleted, the body begins to age, deteriorate, and break down.

Rupert Sheldrake's concept of morphogenetic fields suggests that your thoughts and consciousness shape the energetic patterns that give rise to physical forms. Your thoughts, both past and future, contribute to the energetic blueprint that manifests as your present reality. In this sense, aging is not only a physical process but a reflection of the energy patterns you carry within your bioenergetic field.

The good news? You have the power to influence this energy. Every thought you think and every emotion you feel carries energy that impacts your cells, your DNA, and, ultimately, your physical body. Pain, illness, and aging may simply be manifestations of unresolved thought patterns stored as energy blockages in your DNA. And you don't have to wait for physical symptoms to take action.

Through practices like conscious thought management, meditation, and energy healing, you can intercept and transform these patterns before they manifest in the physical realm. These stored thought forms - tiny energy crystals within your DNA - may inhibit the natural process of DNA regeneration. By consciously transforming this energy, you can begin to reassemble and restore your DNA, unlocking vitality and youthfulness from within.

Sound, Frequency, and the Future of Healing

Emerging research in sound therapy and vibrational medicine provides further insight into the profound connection between energy and physical health. Studies show that specific frequencies can influence cellular processes, heal emotional wounds, and promote deep relaxation. Dr. Jeffrey Thompson, for example, discovered that different parts of the spine resonate at distinct frequencies. Using sound therapy, he has helped align vertebrae, balance organ function, and even enhance immune responses.

These discoveries point to an undeniable truth: your body is not merely a physical entity; it is an intricate energetic system that non-physical elements, such as sound and vibration, can influence. This is the frontier of healing, where the lines between energy, consciousness, and biology blur.

Rethinking Nourishment: It's More than Just Food

It is often taught that food is the sole source of nourishment for your body. If that were true, then why doesn't consuming the "right" foods guarantee eternal health and vitality? The answer lies in the intricate process by which the body transforms food into usable energy. It's not the food itself that nourishes your cells but the energy and intelligence within your body that determines how, and even if, that nourishment reaches your cells.

Imagine biting into a crisp, juicy apple. As you chew, a cascade of biological processes begins, breaking down the apple into nutrients. Enzymes in your saliva transform starches into sugars; gastric juices in your stomach continue the work, breaking down proteins and fibers. By the time the nutrients reach your cells, your body has meticulously filtered, absorbed, and distributed what it needs.

Yet this is just the surface. Beneath it all lies the body's innate wisdom, an energetic intelligence that discerns what to absorb, what to discard, and how to maintain balance. This process goes far beyond mere biology. It's a dance of energy, a symphony of transformation happening in every moment.

True nourishment, then, is more than just food. It is the energy that feeds your cells, your thoughts, and your soul. When you understand how to harness this energy, you unlock the door to ageless vitality. It begins with recognizing that you are more than your physical body. You are energy, and the way you direct, transform, and nourish that energy will determine not only how you age but how you live.

Are you ready to explore the realms beyond the physical?

The Cellular Power Plants: Mitochondria and ATP

Imagine your body as a bustling city, with every cell acting like a tiny factory constantly working to keep the lights on and the systems running smoothly. Just like factories need power, your cells require energy, fuel that powers everything from muscle movement to DNA replication. The fascinating part? This energy isn't ready to use from the food you eat. Instead, it undergoes a miraculous transformation inside your body.

Once nutrients are transported to your cells through the bloodstream, the real magic happens. Carbohydrates, fats, and proteins can't directly power the cell's activities. Like raw materials that need refining before they're useful, these nutrients must be transformed into adenosine triphosphate (ATP). This is the cellular currency of energy.

The mitochondria, often called the "powerhouses of the cell," perform this critical job. Through a process known as cellular respiration, they break down nutrients into ATP. It can be likened to converting coal into electricity, except here, it's your body transforming food into fuel.

Think of ATP as the energy your cells need to carry out their essential functions, much like a rechargeable battery that powers your daily life. From muscle contraction to DNA repair, ATP is central to every function your cells perform. It's the energetic lifeblood that keeps you alive.

Now, here's where things get interesting. While the mitochondria are the key players in energy production, what happens when the quality of your food is compromised? Nutrients laced with additives and carcinogens become like a low-grade fuel, so while your body can use it, the process becomes sluggish, and the results are less than ideal. Imagine running a high-performance sports car on cheap, watered-down gas. Eventually, the engine will stutter, and the performance will falter.

The same happens with your body. When your cells receive substandard nutrients, your energy, vitality, and cellular efficiency plummet. What if there's more to nourishment than just the physical components of food? Could energy, beyond the calories on your plate, play a role in how you fuel your cells?

Let me stretch your perspective further. Imagine each bite of food or sip of water as not just a physical substance but a carrier of energetic frequencies. Every item you consume holds a vibrational signature, from where it was grown and how it was handled to how it has been prepared and plated up. The fresh, vibrant energy of organic fruits and vegetables hum with life, while processed, nutrient-stripped foods carry lower, sluggish frequencies. These energetic frequencies interact with your own body's bioenergetic field, impacting not just your physical health but also your emotional and spiritual well-being.

Much like tuning an instrument, your body resonates with these frequencies, adjusting itself to either harmony or discord based on the quality of energy it receives. The foods you consume become not only fuel for your cells but also a contributor to your energetic frequency.

Beyond Physical Food: Can Your Cells Generate Energy From Pure Consciousness?

Now, let's leap into the extraordinary. What if your body didn't need food to generate energy at all? This idea, which might seem straight out of science fiction, taps into a world of ancient wisdom and cutting-edge theories. Some believe the human body is capable of drawing energy directly from the universe itself, bypassing the need for conventional nourishment. This process is often referred to as "Breatharianism." "Source feeding" or prana-based living.

For centuries, spiritual practitioners and mystics have claimed that human beings can tap into prana—the vital life force that flows through all things. Some, like the mystics Martha Nasch and Teresa Neumann, reportedly survived for years without food or water, relying solely on this energetic sustenance. What if these extraordinary cases were glimpses of an untapped human potential?

Hilton Hotema, in his book *Man's Higher Consciousness*, suggests that humans were originally breatharians—beings sustained purely by prana. His work, along with many other historical and modern examples, raises the provocative question: could we return to this state of being?

One modern-day example is renowned physicist Nassim Haramein, who delved deeply into the practice of Source feeding during his years of ascetic living. Haramein's theories of the universe as an interconnected field of energy suggest that every point in space holds infinite energy accessible to all. His experiences led him to believe that through practices like meditation, breath control, and energy alignment, we can tap into this limitless energy field.

Just a fraction of the energy in a cubic centimeter of quantum space could power the entire world for millennia. So, if the universe is so abundant, perhaps the human body can draw on this energy, too, allowing us to exist in harmony with the cosmos rather than depending solely on physical sustenance.

Beyond Calories, Toward Consciousness

Science has long relied on the calorie-based model of nutrition. Basically, energy in, energy out. However, studies from researchers like Dr. Paul Webb have shown that the human body's energy balance is far more complex. Webb's work suggests that traditional metabolic processes cannot explain up to 23% of the energy produced by the body. Could this "missing" energy come from an unknown source? Could it be that we've only scratched the surface of how our bodies generate and use energy?

Remember, energy cannot be created or destroyed; it only transforms. And if energy is the basis of all things, perhaps the human body can sustain itself on pure energy, bypassing the conventional food system altogether. This opens the door to a radical reimagining of how we nourish ourselves. Through practices like source feeding, there lies the possibility that you can heal your body and transform your relationship with energy and consciousness itself.

As you explore the profound connection between energy, consciousness, and nourishment, it becomes clear that food is not merely sustenance; it is energy.

Could this be the future of human vitality? An existence where we live in harmony with the energetic forces that sustain us, liberated from the limitations of physical sustenance?

Building on the idea that energy is the foundation of all existence, Source feeding through the practice of living off prana emerges as a revolutionary alternative for human nourishment. By lessening dependence on physical food and water, practitioners of Source feeding seek sustenance directly from the universe's boundless energy. This practice, known as a *siddhi* in the ancient *Yoga Sutras*, presents a transformative pathway that bypasses conventional consumption. It aligns deeply with the concept that consciousness itself is a form of energy capable of sustaining life.Unlike fasting, which has seen a resurgence in popularity as a means of detoxifying the body, Source feeding operates on a fundamentally different principle. Fasting is temporary and rooted in the body's physical fuel reserves. When fasting or consuming a low-carbohydrate diet, the body eventually depletes its immediate source of energy, which is glucose. At this point, it shifts to a backup mode, breaking down fats into ketones. These ketones act as an alternative energy source, fueling both the body and the brain in place of glucose. This transition often results in mental clarity that people attribute to fasting; it's as though the brain, suddenly free of its reliance on sugars, enters a heightened state of focus and awareness.

But here's the catch: fasting, while powerful, remains tied to physical fuel sources. It's a biological trick, a survival mechanism. The body consumes stored fat, which sustains it for a time, but eventually, even that reservoir dries up. If pushed too long, fasting leads to muscle atrophy, accelerated aging, and ultimately, death.

The Limitations of Fasting

Science has uncovered the remarkable benefits of food deprivation, which include stem cell regeneration, DNA repair, and even enhanced recovery from diseases like cancer and Alzheimer's. However, fasting comes with a significant limitation: its temporary nature. Your body, though cleansed and rejuvenated, is still bound to the physical reality of food. Even in its most efficient state, fasting relies on stored nutrients and cannot sustain the body indefinitely without a return to solid food. Eventually, the body's energy reservoirs deplete, leading to physical deterioration.

Imagine trying to run an engine on fumes; it may sputter along for a time, but without fuel, it will eventually seize. This is the reality of prolonged fasting. The body, in its wisdom, slows its processes, conserves its energy, and turns inward to maintain survival. But this method has an expiration date.

Source Feeding: Nourishment Beyond the Physical

What if your cells could bypass the need for glucose, fat, or any physical food altogether? Enter Source feeding through prana. In this remarkable process, the body is "fed" and nourished not by breaking down physical substances but by absorbing superior, energetic nourishment from an unseen and seemingly unexplainable source.

To visualize this, think of plants in photosynthesis and how they turn sunlight into energy without needing to consume another living thing. Source feeding takes this one step further. While plants rely on the sun, prana exists everywhere, constantly available in the air, in the light, and in the energy field that surrounds all things. Practitioners of Source feeding tap into this vast, invisible reservoir to sustain themselves.

This nourishment, far from being limited to the physical elements of vitamins or minerals, is thought to come from the very source of existence itself, the pure, omnipresent energy that underpins life. It provides a level of sustenance that not only nourishes the body but also aligns with one's emotional, spiritual, and energetic well-being.

Think of prana as an advanced fuel or solar power in a world where everyone else is burning coal. While others dig into the earth for energy, struggling to sustain themselves through increasingly depleting resources, those who live through prana simply tap into the abundant energy all around them. It's renewable, limitless, and vibrationally harmonious with the body.

What's more intriguing is that this unseen force doesn't just fuel the physical form; it nourishes the mind and spirit in profound ways. When you reduce reliance on physical sustenance, your body becomes more in tune with the flow of energy around you. This alignment can lead to greater mental clarity, emotional balance, and spiritual insight.

Unlike the temporary benefits of fasting, Source feeding through prana holds the potential for a more sustainable form of nourishment, untouched by the limitations of time or physical needs. It invites you to not only survive but thrive, fueled by the same life force that powers the universe.

Prana, as defined by the Merriam-Webster dictionary, is described as "a life breath or vital principle in Vedic and later Hindu religion." This definition only begins to capture the profound significance of prana within spiritual and metaphysical contexts. Prana is not merely a concept; it represents the life-sustaining force that flows through every living being and permeates the entire universe. It is the subtle energy that animates all forms of life, connecting the physical body with the spiritual essence.

This idea of a life force is not unique to Vedic traditions. Across various cultures, this vital energy is recognized by different names, each carrying its own cultural and spiritual connotations. In ancient Greek philosophy, it is known as "pneuma," referring to the breath or spirit. In Polynesian culture, the term "mana" signifies a supernatural force that resides in people, objects, and the natural world. Similarly, in Hebrew, the word "ruach" is used to describe the breath of life or the spirit of God, infusing all of creation. Despite the diversity of names and interpretations, these concepts share a common understanding: prana, in its many forms, is the essence of life itself, the invisible thread that connects all living beings to the cosmos.

Harnessing the Power of Prana: Solar, Air, and Ground Energy

Prana can be harnessed from three primary sources: solar prana, air prana, and ground prana. This understanding opens up a world of possibilities, offering a transformative way to nourish the body without relying solely on physical food. By tapping into the boundless energy available from nature, practitioners of Source feeding nourish themselves energetically, leading to enhanced vitality and well-being.

Solar Prana: Nourishment from the Sun

Solar prana, derived from sunlight, is perhaps the most direct way to infuse your body with energy. Just as plants capture sunlight through chlorophyll, the human body can similarly harness solar energy. While your body doesn't contain chlorophyll, it does have the remarkable ability to convert sunlight into usable energy. Through the skin's exposure to sunlight, solar prana triggers essential biological processes, like the synthesis of vitamin D, which plays a critical role in bone health, immune function, and mood regulation.

Incredibly, molecular biologist William Brown, from the Resonance Academy, has studied human photosynthesis and found that sunlight absorbed by the mitochondria can directly drive the production of ATP, the energy currency of the cell. This process mirrors the way plants convert light into energy, suggesting that humans are capable of harvesting energy from sunlight in a manner similar to photosynthesis.

Even more intriguing is the role of melanin, the pigment responsible for skin color. Researcher Arturo Solis Herrera proposed that melanin, like chlorophyll in plants, may help break down water molecules into hydrogen and oxygen, providing an additional energy source for your cells. This discovery hints that the sun's energy can be transformed within the body to fuel essential functions, challenging the long-held belief that glucose and mitochondria are the primary energy sources for cells.

The practice of *sun gazing* - staring at the sun during sunrise or sunset - is another fascinating method to absorb solar prana. Hira Ratan

Manek (HRM), a well-known sun gazer featured in the documentary *In the Beginning, was Light,* claims that sun gazing allowed him to live without food. His prolonged exposure to sunlight even resulted in an enlarged pineal gland. A small organ in the brain and often referred to as the "seat of the soul," the pineal gland plays a crucial role in regulating sleep-wake cycles and possibly even in opening portals to altered states of awareness through the production of dimethyltryptamine (DMT), sometimes called the "spirit molecule."

Air Prana: Breathing in Vitality

Air prana is absorbed through the lungs via deep, rhythmic breathing and is equally crucial for sustaining life. Your breath, much like the sunlight, carries an energetic charge that nourishes your body on a cellular level. While conventional science understands the lungs as the organ responsible for gas exchange, yogic traditions teach that breathing techniques—like Pranayama—are essential for absorbing prana from the air.

Yogic practices such as *Nadi Shodhana* (alternate nostril breathing) or *Bhastrika* (bellows breath) enhance the absorption of air prana by balancing and energizing the body's energy centers. Deep breathing, rather than shallow breaths, promotes greater prana intake, and when combined with mindfulness and intention, the body's energetic flow can be optimized.

Holistic traditions also propose that the skin, beyond its physical function as a barrier, can absorb subtle pranic energies from the environment. With intention, individuals can learn to facilitate the absorption of air prana through the skin's pores, further enhancing their connection to the life force around them.

Ground Prana: The Earth as an Energy Source

Ground prana is absorbed through the soles of the feet and is amplified by direct contact with the Earth, a practice known as grounding or earthing. Walking barefoot on the earth allows for an efficient transfer of the Earth's energy into the body, nourishing and recharging the system. The Earth carries a negative electrical charge due to its vast reservoir of free electrons. When your bare feet touch the ground, these electrons are absorbed into your body, neutralizing free radicals and reducing inflammation. The documentary *Earthing* explores the profound health benefits of grounding, from improved sleep and immune function to reduced stress and pain.

Ancient indigenous rituals also point to the power of ground prana. In some cultures, healing practices involved burying a person up to their neck in the earth, allowing the individual to draw healing energy directly from the ground. This practice, while rare, reflects the deep connection humans have with the earth's energy and its potential to restore balance and vitality.

Water as a Conduit for Prana

Water, too, is a potent carrier of pranic energy. When exposed to sunlight or allowed to interact with the earth, water absorbs prana, becoming a powerful tool for rejuvenating the body's energy systems. This "living water" is not only physically hydrating but also vibrationally nourishing, charged with energy that supports your physical and spiritual well-being.

Dr. Gerald Pollack, author of *The Fourth Phase of Water*, discovered that water in its fourth phase - H_3O_2 - is more structured and can store sunlight's energy, releasing it as needed by the body. This special form of water, present in your cells, acts as a biological photocell, continuously charged by sunlight. In this way, water becomes an intermediary, allowing your body to store and utilize pranic energy in a highly efficient form.

Integrating Pranic Practices into Daily Life

By consciously engaging with these sources of prana—solar, air, and ground—you can elevate your energy levels and overall well-being. Simple practices like sunbathing, barefoot walking, deep breathing, and drinking sun-charged water can significantly enhance your body's pranic absorption. These practices go beyond nourishing the physical form; they create a deep connection between your body and the abundant energy fields that surround you, offering an expansive and holistic approach to vitality.

As you embrace the idea of prana as a primary source of nourishment, you may find that your reliance on physical food diminishes, replaced by a greater sense of energetic balance, mental clarity, and spiritual alignment. The possibilities are endless—each breath, each step on the earth, and each moment under the sun is an opportunity to infuse your body with the life force that sustains all things.

Re-Imagine
YOU

Here are four short 'how-to' exercises to incorporate Energy Nourishment into daily practice:

Sun-Gazing

Sun-gazing is a practice that allows you to absorb pranic energy directly from the sun, enhancing your vitality and well-being.

How to:

- o **Timing:** Perform sun-gazing within the first hour after sunrise or the last hour before sunset, when the sun's rays are gentle and safe for your eyes.
- o **Positioning:** Stand or sit comfortably, facing the sun. Keep your eyes relaxed and gently open, gazing at the sun without straining.
- o **Duration:** Start with just 10 seconds of gazing on your first day. Gradually increase by 10 seconds each day, working your way up to several minutes.
- o **Breathing:** Inhale deeply and slowly through your nose as you gaze at the sun. Feel the warmth and energy of the sun entering your body with each breath.
- o **Post-Practice:** After sun-gazing, close your eyes and sit quietly for a few minutes, visualizing the sunlight energizing every cell in your body.

Earthing Practice

Earthing, or grounding, connects you to the earth's energy, helping to balance your body's energy system.

How to:

- o **Go Barefoot:** Find a natural area with grass, soil, sand, or stone. Remove your shoes and socks.
- o **Stand or Sit:** Stand or sit with your bare feet in direct contact with the earth. Feel the texture and temperature beneath your feet.

- o **Relax and Connect:** Close your eyes, take a few deep breaths, and focus on the connection between your body and the earth.
- o **Visualize:** Imagine roots growing from the soles of your feet into the earth, drawing up the earth's nourishing energy into your body.
- o **Duration:** Stay in this position for at least 10-20 minutes, allowing the earth's energy to balance and replenish you.

Energizing Water

Energized water is infused with prana, enhancing its ability to nourish and cleanse your body.

How to:

- o **Choose Your Water:** Use pure, natural water, such as spring water or filtered water.
- o **Sun Exposure:** Place the water in a clear glass container and set it in direct sunlight for 1-3 hours, allowing it to absorb the sun's prana.
- o **Intention Setting:** As the water sits in the sun, hold your hands over the container and set a positive intention, such as "This water is filled with life-giving energy."
- o **Consume:** After the water has been charged, drink it slowly, visualizing the prana flowing into your body, replenishing and energizing every cell.

These exercises are designed to help you tap into natural sources of prana, supporting your journey toward energy nourishment and overall well-being.

> "The rejuvenating power of nature lies in its simplicity—sun gazing fills us with the purest light, air prana breathes life into our cells, and earthing connects us to the Earth's healing energy. Together, these practices restore our natural vitality, grounding us in the essence of life itself."

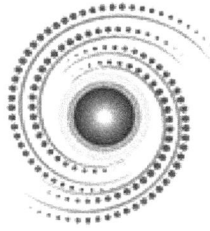

Chapter Eight
Transitioning to Source Feeding

KEY QUESTIONS:

Is it possible to nourish yourself from Prana?
Are there different levels of Source Feeding?

Imagine a distant world, one where towering cities shimmer in the light of multiple suns, and the people who inhabit this world possess an energy unlike anything you have ever known. They live without hunger, without fatigue, and the need for physical sustenance. Their bodies radiate with a vitality that defies time, as if they are nourished not by food but by the very fabric of the universe itself.

Their secret? They have mastered the ancient art of Source feeding, drawing their nourishment directly from the energy around them—light, air, and the Earth's magnetic fields. They understand that true sustenance comes not from what you physically consume but from how you align your body with the life force that flows through everything.

This world might sound like something out of a futuristic novel, yet it is not fiction. These practices have been passed down through the ages, and they are happening now here on Earth.

As I mentioned at the beginning of this book, the Masters of the Far East, chronicled in Baird T. Spalding's writings, lived with this knowledge for millennia, embodying the very principles of energy and life force that we are now rediscovering. These enlightened beings, residing high in remote mountains, had transcended the need for physical sustenance, drawing instead from prana. Their understanding of energy was profound, allowing them to live without food or water, sustained solely by this cosmic force. Their vitality, untouched by time, stands as a testament to the boundless potential of the human body when it aligns with the energy of the universe—reminding us of the ancient truths we explored at the outset of this book, where the limitations of the physical begin to dissolve in the face of true mastery.

Far from being a futuristic fantasy, Source feeding is an ancient practice that has survived the test of time, and more and more people are rediscovering this incredible way of living today. As you delve deeper into this chapter, consider the possibility that we are on the verge of remembering a forgotten truth about the nature of nourishment and what it means to live in harmony with the energy that sustains all life.

The journey toward Source feeding is a shift in both mindset and physiology—a transformation that opens the door to untapped human potential. It challenges the very foundation of modern nutrition and explores deeper connections between energy, consciousness, and physical form.

A Global Movement: The Rise of Source Feeding

Despite the controversy surrounding Source feeding, the number of practitioners has steadily grown over recent decades. According to various reports, over 200,000 individuals worldwide are either fully nourished by prana or are transitioning toward this lifestyle.

Jasmuheen, one of the most prominent advocates for pranic living, explains in her book, *Ambassadors of Light*, that Source feeding is a spiritual initiation and an awakening to the profound reality that nourishment can come from non-physical sources. Jasmuheen's survey of 500 individuals practicing this lifestyle revealed several common characteristics, including regular meditation, a belief in a self-created reality, and a strong commitment to planetary well-being. These individuals hail from a variety of backgrounds—doctors, musicians, businesspeople, and retirees—with a shared understanding that Source feeding goes beyond just food. It is a holistic journey deeply tied to one's spiritual, emotional, and mental health.

Source feeding is not about deprivation; it's about freedom – the freedom to choose how you nourish your body, mind, and soul. Consider, for a moment, living without the need to eat, untethered from the cravings that so often dictate your day-to-day life, feeling fully satiated and no longer bound to the repetitive cycle of hunger, meals, and indulgence. Instead, you find a new kind of freedom that allows you to decide consciously when and if you want to eat.

Contrary to popular belief, many who embrace source feeding do not live a life of restriction. In fact, there are different levels of Source feeding to consider and choose from.

Why Do We Eat? The Hidden Reasons Behind Hunger

Before you can fully appreciate the freedom of Source feeding, it's essential to ask a fundamental question: *Why do you eat?* On the surface, the answer seems simple. You eat to fuel your body. Yet, in truth, the reasons you reach for food are most likely far more complex, woven into your emotions, habits, social dynamics, and cultural conditioning.

Here are some of the most common reasons people eat and how Source feeding can liberate us from these ingrained patterns:

1. **Physical Hunger**: The most obvious reason, of course, is to satisfy physical hunger. However, even this basic instinct is influenced by more than just the body's need for sustenance. It's a conditioned response driven by a lifetime of eating at certain times, in certain amounts, and with certain expectations.

2. **Emotional Eating**: How often have you reached for a snack to soothe stress, boredom, or sadness? Many people use food as an emotional balm, seeking comfort in the act of eating. Whether it's ice cream after a long day or a celebratory meal to

mark an achievement, food becomes a stand-in for emotional fulfillment. Source feeding frees you from this cycle, offering a deeper connection to the emotions themselves without the need to mask them with food.

3. **Social Connections**: Food is a centerpiece of social gatherings. From family dinners to holiday feasts, we bond over shared meals. While this can be a beautiful tradition, it can also become a limiting expectation where every social event revolves around eating. Source-fed individuals discover that true connection goes beyond the dinner table. By detaching from the social pressure to eat, you can engage in more meaningful interactions that focus on presence and conversation rather than consumption.

4. **Cultural and Habitual Patterns**: Many eating habits are dictated by cultural norms. Breakfast, lunch, and dinner at designated times and snacks in between are all based on societal expectations rather than the body's actual needs. These routines are so deeply ingrained that we often eat out of habit rather than hunger. Source feeding offers the freedom to break these patterns, allowing you to nourish your body in a way that feels intuitive, not prescribed.

5. **Cravings and Addiction**: Perhaps the most challenging aspect of eating to break free from is the world of cravings and addiction. Many foods, especially those processed and filled with additives, trigger chemical reactions in the brain that mimic addiction. Sugar, salt, and fat create dopamine spikes, which encourage us to keep eating even when we're full. The liberation of Source feeding comes when you realize that these cravings are not your true desires. By releasing the need for these addictive substances, you free yourself from the constant cycle of wanting more.

Detaching from the Need for Food: The Ultimate Freedom

At its core, Source feeding is about detaching from the deeply rooted belief that you need food to survive.

For many, the transition to Source feeding begins as a gradual journey. Some might start by detoxifying their bodies, reducing their intake of harmful foods, and replacing them with lighter, more energetic options like fruits, vegetables, or juice. Over time, as their connection to prana strengthens, they begin to rely less and less on physical sustenance.

By minimizing exposure to environmental toxins, processed foods, and artificial substances, breatharians reduce the risk of DNA damage and other health issues that arise from conventional eating habits. When the task of constantly digesting food no longer burdens the body, it becomes free to heal, rejuvenate, and regenerate at a cellular level. This freedom from food opens the door to a heightened state of vitality, mental clarity, and emotional balance.

It's important to remember that Source feeding is not a 'one-size-fits-all' journey. There are varying levels of pranic living, and it's a deeply personal experience. For some, Source feeding means living entirely without physical food or water, while for others, it's a blend of pranic nourishment with occasional tastes of physical food. The key is that the choice is yours.

Imagine the freedom of knowing that you are not dependent on food. You may choose to drink water or have a small taste of your favorite meal, but there's no urgency behind it and no craving or insatiable need. This shift in perspective is transformative. It opens the door to a new way of relating to your body and its energy, where you are no longer enslaved by hunger or the constant search for your next meal.

In our modern world, the idea of living without food challenges everything you've been taught about survival, nutrition, and health. But Source feeding is not about denying yourself or suffering through hunger. It's about accessing a new kind of nourishment—one that is always available, abundant, and completely free. It's a shift from external dependency to internal empowerment, from consumption to connection.

A Life Untethered

Consider, for a moment, what your life might be like if you were no longer tethered to food. The freedom to live without the constant need for meals, the cravings that pull you in different directions, or the emotional ties to eating. What would you do with that extra time, energy, and clarity?

For those who embark on the path of Source feeding, the rewards are profound. They speak of enhanced mental clarity, increased energy levels, deeper spiritual growth, and an extraordinary sense of liberation from the physical world. When you no longer *need* food, you open up new possibilities for your life. You gain the freedom to explore higher states of consciousness, access deeper levels of creativity, and connect more fully with your true self.

And perhaps, most importantly, you realize that true nourishment doesn't come from what you consume but from the energy that already flows within you. Source feeding is a reminder that the most profound source of sustenance is not found on your plate but in the boundless energy of the universe, always waiting to nourish you if only you choose to receive it.

The Levels of Source Feeding: A Gradual Evolution

Level 4: The True Breatharians

At the highest level of Source feeding are the true breatharians, a rare and extraordinary group that represents perhaps one in every ten million people. These individuals live in a "dry mode," meaning they do not consume food or water for extended periods, sometimes for years. Their digestive systems operate at a minimal capacity of about 0.1-1% of the time. Likely living in remote areas away from the bustle of society, they have mastered the art of drawing water from the air itself, allowing them to survive without traditional nourishment.

One of the most notable examples of a Level 4 breatharian is Prahlad Jani, an Indian yogi who claimed to live without food or water for decades. His assertions caught the attention of the scientific community, and in 2003, he volunteered for a study in India where he was monitored around the clock for 10 days. Remarkably, Jani showed no signs of dehydration or malnutrition, and his body appeared to recycle urine internally. While his claims sparked skepticism, the findings challenged conventional wisdom and hinted at the incredible potential of the human body.

Level 3: Living with Minimal Sustenance

Most breatharians, or pranic living practitioners, fall under Level 3. These individuals consume liquids or small amounts of food on occasion, but they can go for weeks or even months, subsisting solely on water or nothing at all. Their digestive systems function only 10-30% of the time, and they have usually undergone an initiation process, such as the well-known 21-day program.

Ray Maor, a prominent Level 3 breatharian, underwent a 21-day initiation process that included seven days of dry fasting, followed by seven days of water fasting and another week of diluted juices. To prove the legitimacy of his practice, Maor agreed to an experiment where he went eight days without food or water under strict medical observation. The results were astounding. He lost no weight, had normal blood chemistry, and demonstrated no adverse effects.

Level 2: The Transitionary Stage

Level 2 breatharians are those in the process of integrating pranic living into their daily lives. After undergoing an initiation, it can take several months for the body to fully adapt to this new way of being. Many Level 2 practitioners still consume some solid food, but they are committed to a healthy lifestyle and experience profound improvements in consciousness, health, and happiness. Their digestive systems operate 40-60% of the time, and they often incorporate intermittent fasting into their routine.

Level 1: A Step Toward Healthier Living

At the entry-level of pranic living, people may not be ready to give up food entirely, but they are interested in improving their health. Many Level 1 practitioners are vegetarians, vegans, or intermittent fasters who detoxify regularly. They are working to shift their relationship with food and lay the groundwork for deeper spiritual and physical transformation.

Scientific Perspectives: A New Frontier of Understanding

While scientific research on Source feeding remains limited, some studies on intermittent fasting and extreme calorie restriction have shown intriguing benefits. For instance, a study of individuals fasting for 30 consecutive days revealed enhanced immune function, improved cognitive abilities, and a reduction in cancer and neurodegenerative disease markers.

Even more exciting is the possibility that the body can adapt to live without food through processes we are just beginning to understand.

Jasmuheen, who has lived as a pranic being for over 30 years, believes that pranic living is not for everyone. She strongly advises individuals to undergo testing before attempting to live purely on prana. She suggests breath tests and kinesiology can help determine if someone is ready for this transformation.

Whether you choose to fully embrace pranic living or simply integrate aspects of it into your life, Source feeding offers a pathway toward freedom to redefine nourishment, elevate your consciousness, and explore the limitless potential of the human spirit.

As you consider the possibilities of Source feeding, ask yourself: What truly nourishes you? Could you live from the life force that permeates the universe, breaking free from the physical limitations of food? The answers may surprise you. Whether you pursue pranic living or simply wish to improve your health, the principles of Source feeding invite you to reimagine your relationship with nourishment—and, ultimately, with life itself.

Re-Imagine
YOU

In the instant of your first breath, you are infused with the single greatest force in the universe: the power to translate the possibilities of your thoughts into the reality of your world. To fully awaken your powers may require a subtle change in the way you think of yourself and a shift in belief. Beliefs are those convictions that you hold as being true and trust as being true. Simply put, a belief is a thought that is thought over and over again. What makes a belief true or real is that you have to believe it intellectually, and you have to believe it emotionally. If only you think the thought intellectually, it is just an idea. If you only think about the thought emotionally, then it is just a feeling. When the belief is held in your thoughts and feelings, it becomes true for you. It does not necessarily mean that it is right or even that it is true.

Your beliefs shape the lens through which you perceive and interact with the world, influencing every aspect of your life—from your sense of self to your relationships, health, and even the food you choose to nourish your body. As you become more aware of the power of your thoughts and the beliefs they create, you open the door to profound transformation.

This awareness invites you to take a moment to reflect on the beliefs you hold, particularly those surrounding nourishment and eating. Consider these questions as a starting point for that reflection:

o   What do you believe about the role of food in your life?

o   How were you taught to view food and eating as a child?

o   Do you associate certain foods with specific emotions or memories? If so, what are they?

o   How do you feel about the idea of eating for nourishment versus eating for pleasure?

- o What do you think would happen if you changed your eating habits drastically?

- o Do you believe that certain foods are inherently "good" or "bad"? Why?

- o How do you perceive your relationship with food? Is it nurturing, controlling, or something else?

- o What cultural or societal messages about food and eating have influenced you the most?

"Imagine going beyond the boundaries of who you believe yourself to be... and opening up to new possibilities."

PART FOUR
SUMMARY

- Your cells do not directly absorb nutrients from the food you consume. Instead, you employ a complicated system to break down food into smaller, usable components that can be utilized by the cells to maintain and repair your system.

- Food and drinks laden with additives and potential carcinogens impair cellular functions and the body's ability to convert food into energy efficiently.

- Each substance carries its unique energetic signature that, when ingested, interacts with your bioenergetic field, influencing your physical, emotional, and spiritual well-being.

- Source Feeding advocates a holistic approach to nourishing the body, emphasizing the importance of mindful consumption and energetic resonance with nutritive elements.

- The human body is remarkably adaptive and resourceful when it comes to acquiring the nutrients it needs to function optimally.

- Experimental evidence shows that light imparts energy to water, including body water, and that energy may, in some instances, provide enough energy to sustain life.

- Source feeding offers numerous benefits physically, emotionally, mentally, and spiritually, including enhanced vitality, mental clarity, less requirement for sleep, enhanced creativity, and more spiritual growth.

Embarking on the Path of Source Feeding
Personal Journeys, Collective Insights, and Conclusive Perspectives

That moment, where sight slipped away, and the vast unknown enveloped me, echoes in this chapter. Darkness so often feared and yet so frequently misunderstood, became my gateway to something greater. It's the place where the unseen thrives, where the deepest parts of ourselves are revealed.

As a child, the night light was my lifeline, a fragile barrier against the monsters I was convinced lurked just beyond the shadows. Darkness was painted as a realm of threats and ghosts, ghouls, and everything unseen. It was where the mind filled the unknown with terror.

But what if darkness was never something to fear? What if, instead, it held the key to untold potential, the very thing we've been conditioned to avoid and yet need to embrace?

Both upbringing and culture often program us to associate light with safety and purity while darkness is shrouded in danger and mystery. This conditioning runs so deep that even as adults, we shy away from the dark, equating it with uncertainty and harm. Yet, darkness is as essential as light. It's not just a space of rest and renewal; it is where the most profound growth occurs. Seeds germinate in the dark soil; stars are born in the blackness of space. And it is in the dark that we are invited to dive inward, confronting the hidden aspects of ourselves that light often obscures.

Imagine a hidden tribe high in Colombia's mystical Sierra Nevada mountains, where the journey to enlightenment begins in pure, unbroken darkness. Known as the Mamos, these spiritual guardians handpick children from birth through divine rites, plunging them into a life veiled in shadow. For nine years, these chosen ones live in total darkness, guided only by the whispers of their elders, and are fed a diet crafted to harmonize them with Aluna, the mysterious force believed to be the source of all creation. For some, the path does not end there. If deemed worthy, they return to the darkness for another nine years. Eighteen years, devoid of light, isolated from the visible world, all to master the unseen realms and emerge as powerful intermediaries between Spirit and matter.

This isn't a legend. It's a living reality unfolding right now, where darkness is a sacred womb and where transformation, initiation, and enlightenment take root. Here, what's hidden awakens, and the unseen becomes a force of boundless power.

From the caves of ancient Greece, where seekers journeyed into darkness to access divine knowledge, to the Taoist sages who retreated into the Earth to tap into the essence of life, the dark has always been revered as a sacred space of discovery. Even in Buddhism, darkness is used as a metaphor for the end of suffering as well as a time of gestation where the soul finds light through the shadows.

In every tradition, darkness holds the promise of something greater. It is the paradoxical birthplace of light. "When you go into the dark, and this becomes total, the darkness soon turns into light," says the Tao. What once seemed threatening becomes illuminating.

Darkness as a Catalyst for Detox and Transformation

Stepping into the dark is not just about switching off from physical food; it is the starting point for a far deeper detox—a mental, emotional, physical, and spiritual purification. The darkness or a darkroom retreat acts as a powerful catalyst, stripping away the distractions of the outside world and forcing you to confront what lies beneath. It is in the absence of external light that the internal light begins to emerge, illuminating the layers of conditioning and attachment we carry.

For those seeking to be source-fed, the journey is not merely about removing food from the equation. It requires a massive mental detox, shutting off from the mass conditioning, societal programs, and the beliefs that have dictated how and why we eat. We've been trained to equate food with survival, comfort, and even identity—the emotional ties to food run deep. We eat to soothe our fears, to celebrate, to connect socially, and often, to fill voids we don't fully understand.

In the darkness, these emotional connections are brought to the surface. The absence of food reveals the patterns we've clung to—patterns of craving, addiction, and attachment. It becomes a journey of unlearning, of shedding the layers that have kept us tethered to physical sustenance. The darkness allows for a reset of the mind and emotions, creating space for new connections to be made - connections to prana, the life force that sustains everything.

This process is profound and transformative. It's not just about letting go of food; it's about letting go of the illusions we've been taught about nourishment. When you detach from these emotional and mental constructs, you begin to open yourself to a different kind of sustenance- one that comes not from the outside but from within. Darkness becomes the doorway to freedom, the starting point of Source feeding, where the body, mind, and spirit are re-tuned to a higher frequency of nourishment.

So, I ask you: *Are you still afraid of the dark?* Or are you ready to step into it, switch off the external world, and embrace the profound inner journey it offers?

As you'll discover in the next chapter, the darkness—far from being something to fear—can be warm, inviting, and deeply nourishing. It is where true Source feeding begins, where the body, mind, and spirit align with the cosmic energy that sustains all things.

Re-Imagine **YOU**

Chapter Nine

A Personal Journey into Dark Room
Technology and Source Feeding

KEY QUESTIONS:

How can darkness assist you in healing and spiritual growth?
What happens when you spend extended time in darkness?

Envision a space where you are enveloped in pure darkness. This is not the kind of darkness you experience when you close your eyes; it is a complete absence of light, where every sense you rely on fades away. Neither the darkness of fear nor nightfall; this is the darkness that holds secrets, wisdom, and the potential for transformation. This is the kind of darkness where reality shifts, time bends, and the boundaries between what you know and what you've never imagined begin to blur.

Stepping into a dark room, devoid of all external stimulation, felt like stepping out of the world I knew and into an entirely different dimension. I wasn't just disconnecting from the light. I was disconnecting from everything familiar, from the rules that governed my daily life, and from the constant mental chatter that accompanies the daily grind. This was a space where something deeper awaited—a chance to explore the farthest reaches of perception, to shed the limits of physical existence, and perhaps to discover the limitless potential within.

I've spent much of my life pushing the boundaries of what is considered normal when it comes to health, nourishment, and human potential. For over forty years, my commitment to a vegetarian and vegan lifestyle gradually evolved into an exploration of lighter and lighter forms of nourishment. By the time I encountered the concept of Breatharianism and Dark Room Technology in 2016, my curiosity was piqued. But it wasn't until 2019 that I truly felt ready to immerse myself in this paradigm shift in nourishment. It seemed impossible by conventional standards but fascinatingly aligned with my vision of what the human body could achieve.

The COVID-19 pandemic delayed my plans, but by March 2023, I found myself in Thailand, ready to begin an immersive exploration of Dark Room Technology and Source feeding. Under the guidance of Jasmuheen, one of the world's foremost proponents of this alternative lifestyle, I entered a purpose-built darkroom facility designed to facilitate a deep connection with pranic energy. It was a nine-day journey into total darkness, with only water or fresh juice available if needed. The preparation for this journey was just as intense, including months of parasite cleansing, regular water fasting, and a gradual shift to a lighter diet, paving the way for what was to come.

This wasn't just about removing food. It was about stepping into a world where light itself no longer existed and where the body, mind, and spirit were invited to reconnect with something far more fundamental—the energy that flows through all things.

Darkness as a Portal

It was astonishing to witness how swiftly one adapts to complete darkness, as if the body and mind had always known the way. By the third day, I found myself effortlessly navigating the room, sensing the space with a precision I hadn't imagined. What initially felt disorienting quickly turned into an embrace of stillness, revealing how comfortable the unknown can become with time. I'd always been the type to thrive on *doing*, but here, in the Darkroom, I discovered the profound beauty of simply *being*. The me from years ago might have felt restless or even imprisoned by such quiet solitude, yet in this moment, I felt liberated. Each time the gong reverberated through the dark, it reluctantly pulled me from deep meditations, vivid dreams, and contemplative states that felt as expansive as the universe itself back into the powerful group gatherings in the Darkroom central space.

When you spend extended time in darkness, something extraordinary happens. The first thing you notice is the absence—not just of light, but of all the external stimuli that usually flood your senses. In the silence and stillness, the mind begins to shift. Sensory deprivation acts as a gateway to deeper layers of awareness, peeling away the superficial thoughts and emotions that normally dominate our consciousness.

In this state, I found myself diving into a space where the usual boundaries of time and space no longer held sway. It felt as though I was touching something beyond the physical world—a place where the limitations of the body began to dissolve, and a new connection to energy, to prana, began to take form.

Just like the story of *Sleeping Beauty*, who fell into a deep slumber, waiting for the moment of her awakening, the body, too, enters a period of profound rest and rejuvenation under the influence of melatonin. This "sleep hormone," often associated with regulating our circadian rhythms, becomes the key to unlocking deeper layers of healing and regeneration.

Just as Sleeping Beauty lay still, protected from the outside world, her body quietly working to maintain her vitality, melatonin puts your body into a state of deep repair. Extended periods of darkness stimulate the production of this hormone, which not only helps with sleep but also plays a crucial role in DNA repair and cellular restoration. In essence, melatonin is the prince that "awakens" your cells, rejuvenating them after a prolonged period of rest.

Research shows that melatonin has a powerful effect on mitochondrial function, boosting ATP production—the energy that fuels every cell in the body. In the dark, melatonin takes center stage. It enhances the body's ability to thrive without physical sustenance, acting as a natural bridge between rest, repair, and nourishment.

The dance of hunger within the body is led by two powerful hormones: Ghrelin and Leptin. Ghrelin, often dubbed the "hunger whisperer," originates mainly from the stomach, sounding the alarm when it's empty and quieting down once it's filled. Imagine it as a signal flare, alerting the brain that fuel is needed. Once food stretches the stomach, the flare is extinguished, and the hunger subsides.

Leptin, on the other hand, plays a more subtle role, like a quiet overseer in the brain's appetite center. It binds to receptors, moderating brain cells to balance energy intake. When Leptin levels rise, they suppress hunger while nudging the body to burn stored fat, like a conductor guiding an orchestra to shift tempo. The more Leptin in your system, the more it whispers to your brain, "You've had enough."

Interestingly, Melatonin joins this dance as well. Studies show it positively influences Leptin levels, adding an unexpected layer to hunger suppression, particularly during periods of rest. This connection reveals why extended time in a Darkroom, with its meditative tranquility, has such profound effects. In 2012, a study published in *Frontiers in Neurology* found that experienced meditators had melatonin levels 500% higher than non-meditators, offering a scientific glimpse into the rejuvenating power of meditation and its deeper relationship to hunger and energy regulation.

Much like Sleeping Beauty, it transforms during the quiet hours of slumber. These extended rest and meditations are not passive states but active processes where the body rejuvenates, detoxifies, and prepares itself for awakening stronger and more nourished than before.

Darkness doesn't just impact the body; it triggers a profound transformation in consciousness. Taoist master Mantak Chia describes the stages of this journey, where melatonin production reaches a peak, followed by the release of Pinoline. This neurotransmitter enhances dream states, intuition, and spiritual awareness. As time in the dark increases, the body begins to produce 5-MeO-DMT—a psychoactive compound that awakens the nervous system, activating heightened emotional and intuitive experiences.

At this point, darkness becomes light. The mind begins to perceive flashes of illumination, even though there is no external source of light. I remember vividly lying in the dark and feeling as though a brilliant disco ball was spinning above me, radiating beams of light. But when I opened my eyes, there was only blackness. This is the threshold where the darkness begins to reveal its true nature - an inner light that emerges from the depths of our own consciousness.

While fasting has been linked to increased production of endogenous DMT, some breatharians report experiencing altered states of consciousness, including visions, auditory experiences, and other forms of extrasensory perception, similar to the effects of DMT. One notable example is Peter Aziz, who documents his experiences in a book titled Breatharianism: The Art of Living Without Food. Jasmuheen also shared a range of spiritual and mystical experiences during the Darkroom experience.

Perhaps the most transformative aspect of the darkroom experience was the profound detox that took place—not just physically but mentally and emotionally. In the absence of food and light, I was confronted with the deep-seated attachments that had governed much of my life. The desire for food, the emotional ties to eating, the societal conditioning that equates nourishment with consumption—all of these patterns rose to the surface.

In the silence of the dark, I was able to observe these attachments without judgment, allowing them to dissolve naturally. The emotional detox was as powerful as the physical one. As the days passed, I found myself letting go of cravings, desires, and the need to fill myself with external things. Instead, I began to connect with the internal source of energy that had always been there, waiting to be tapped into.

Delving Deeper
More than just a retreat, the Darkroom experience was an accelerated leap in self-evolution. It peeled back layers of accumulated imprints,

those energy stamps embedded in the cellular memory—patterns from this life and traces from others. As each day passed in the deep darkness, memories surfaced unbidden, drawing me back through the corridors of time. It felt as if I were systematically reviewing my entire existence, from childhood to the present and even beyond. This process can be likened to what anthropologist Carlos Castaneda describes as 'recapitulation.' It was a cleansing of energetic ties, a release of unresolved interactions that had woven themselves into my DNA.

The ancient Mexican Shamans that Castaneda encountered taught that recapitulation was not just remembering but reliving and a complete re-experiencing of every significant moment, person, and event. In their view, this was a way to reclaim energy, to unhook yourself from the energetic webs that drain your vitality. Imagine every argument and every emotional encounter as an exchange of energy. The more intense the moment, the greater the energetic toll. Have you ever felt completely drained after a difficult conversation? That's the energy loss the Shamans spoke of and the energy left behind in the fragments of those interactions.

These fragments, stored within our cells, function like scenes from a film etched into our DNA. They are part of the cellular memory, constantly replaying until they are healed. What was most fascinating during the Darkroom process was that these imprints weren't just from this lifetime. They reached across time, linking past and future selves, all coexisting simultaneously within the multidimensional fabric of the DNA. As I healed the memories of my present, I felt the ripple effect traveling through time, altering the course of my past and shaping new potential futures.

It's here, within the dormant portions of our intron DNA, that our most profound memories reside, untapped and waiting. With each memory drawn to the surface and healed, I began to access deeper layers of race memory, connecting not only to my personal story but to the greater story of humanity. The Darkroom was a gateway, a portal to the multidimensional self that exists across time, space, and beyond, revealing that we are far more than we realize. In those quiet, dark moments, the blueprint of my DNA was evolving, unfolding the greater truth of who I really am.

Rebirth and Renewal

When it was finally time to leave, stepping out into the world felt like emerging from a cocoon, bathed in a tidal wave of emotion I could never adequately describe. It wasn't just a return; it was a rebirth. Gratitude filled every cell of my body. While many of my companions immediately craved the grounding sensation of solid food, I found myself lingering in the in-between, gently transitioning over the months that followed with raw foods and diluted juices. The experience had profoundly shifted my relationship with nourishment, both physically and energetically, nudging me towards a deeper connection with Source feeding.

For months after the experience, I continued with a simplified form of nourishment, which included diluted juices, deuterium-depleted water, and regular sun-gazing. The dark room fundamentally changed my relationship with food and energy. I no longer needed food in the same way, and the connection to prana, to the energy that sustains all life, became my primary source of nourishment.

My journey into Dark Room Technology and Source feeding is far from over. It has opened the door to a way of living that transcends the boundaries of what we consider possible. As I continue to explore the possibilities of pranic living, I invite you, the reader, to question what it means to nourish yourself truly.

Re-Imagine
YOU

To explore the sensory and perceptual abilities of the body and mind in complete darkness, including the potential to navigate without sight and to sense colors or shapes beyond ordinary vision, purchase a Mindfold blackout sleeping mask and choose a room where you can create total darkness. Ensure that all light sources, including electronics, are turned off or covered, clear any obstacles from the floor, and create a safe, uncluttered area where you can move around freely. Place a few objects (soft or non-sharp) in different parts of the room.

- Before entering the dark space, set an intention to explore and expand your sensory awareness beyond ordinary sight. Affirm your openness to perceiving the environment in new ways.

- Step into the darkened room and take a few moments to stand or sit quietly, allowing your body and mind to adjust to the absence of light. Focus on your breath and relax.

- Begin by tuning into your other senses. Notice the sounds, the feel of the air on your skin, and the subtle sensations in your body. Take slow, deep breaths to calm your mind and enhance your sensory awareness.

- Slowly start to move around the space, using your hands to explore your surroundings gently. Allow your body to navigate instinctively without relying on sight. Pay attention to how your body and mind start to compensate for the lack of vision. Trust your other senses to guide you.

- Once you are comfortable moving in the darkness, pause and focus on your inner vision. Imagine the objects in the room, sensing their shapes, colors, or energy fields with your mind's eye.

- After spending some time navigating and sensing in the darkness, return to a still position. Close your eyes, even in the dark, and take a few deep breaths. Reflect on any sensations or experiences you had during the exercise.

- When you're ready to end the exercise, slowly reintroduce light into the room. Open your eyes gently, allowing them to adjust gradually.

Reflection: Consider what it was like to move in complete darkness and whether you were able to perceive shapes, colors, or other sensory information without sight. Reflect on how this practice might enhance your intuition or other sensory abilities over time.

"In the embrace of darkness, we find the space where true clarity emerges. It is within the shadows that our deepest insights are illuminated, revealing the unseen and awakening the dormant powers of our inner vision."

Re-Imagine **YOU**

Chapter Ten

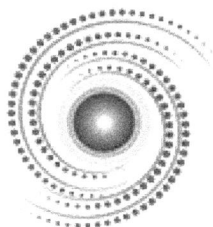

The Alchemy of Dry Fasting:
Pranic Living Retreat

KEY QUESTIONS:

Does eating hinder the healing process?
What is the difference between exogenous water and
endogenous water?

Picture this: the lone wanderer, stumbling through an unforgiving desert, lips cracked, eyes squinting under the relentless sun, desperate for a drop of water. In their final moments, an oasis appears in the distance, shimmering like a mirage; hope flickers, only to cruelly vanish. Scenes like these in movies have imprinted the idea that without water, death is inevitable. The message is clear. Three days without water, and the body begins to shut down, succumbing to the elements.

This belief is so deeply embedded in our collective psyche that it feels almost unbreakable, like an irrefutable law of nature. So why was I, a rational, educated person, stepping into a retreat where I would deliberately go without water for four days? Why was I preparing to blow this conditioning to pieces, challenging the very belief that you can't survive beyond that sacred 72-hour mark?

 I wasn't walking into this retreat blindly. This wasn't a reckless attempt to test my physical limits; rather, it was a spiritual and scientific exploration into an alternative reality, one where the body is capable of far more than we've been led to believe. In my first pranic living retreat, I had already begun exploring nourishment beyond food. This second retreat would take it further, beyond even water itself.

The idea that we are entirely dependent on external sources such as food and water for survival is so deeply woven into our biology and culture that it feels dangerous even to question it. Yet, here I was, about to unravel decades of conditioning, stepping into a place where the absence of water wasn't a threat to life but a gateway to deeper healing and understanding of the body's true potential.

I was about to confront the same primal fear we've seen played out in countless survival films where thirst equals death. But instead of succumbing to the fear of the dry, barren desert, I would be exploring an inner oasis, one that promised to nourish me from within. The question wasn't whether I could survive without water for four days; it was whether I could break through the psychological walls that insisted I couldn't.

Unlike my first experience, which revolved around Darkroom Technology, this second retreat was another exploration of making the physical switch to nourishment beyond food and included four days of dry fasting. The shift from being sustained by physical food to an alternative source of nourishment felt like standing on the edge of a cliff, ready to leap into the unknown.

The Shift to Dry Fasting

Preparation for the dry fasting phase began a week prior with a transition to a raw food diet, a familiar process in cleansing the body's internal environment. I took this further by incorporating a personal protocol of parasite cleansing, preparing not just the physical body but also energetically clearing spaces within. Once the retreat began, we progressed gradually: one day of juice, followed by water only, and then into the dry fasting phase of four days without any food or liquid. With my body accustomed to a clean internal state, I avoided the usual detox symptoms, such as headaches that plague many newcomers, especially those accustomed to caffeine or heavily processed diets. Yet, the dry fast wasn't without its challenges. My body screamed for rest, with fatigue draping over me like a heavy blanket. My mouth felt like desert sand, dry within seconds of rinsing my mouth or brushing my teeth. The cold environment of the retreat facility only added to the physical discomfort, intensifying the experience.

Emotional ebbs accompanied the physical symptoms that seemed to mirror the body's cleansing process. Waves of agitation, then peace; exhaustion, then sudden clarity. It felt as though years of stored emotions were finally being given a voice, bubbling to the surface for release. And beneath this, a quiet strength began to emerge.

Engaging in light yoga and Vipassana meditation became vital anchors during this time. These practices helped me tune into my body, allowing space for introspection, rest, and the gradual awakening of a heightened awareness. It was as though this abstinence from food and water opened the doors to higher sensory perception, inviting the wisdom of the body's innate healing mechanisms to take center stage.

Awakening the Body's Inner Resources

One of the most fascinating revelations was the shift from relying on exogenous water (liquid consumed from external sources) to the body's ability to generate endogenous water. As I moved deeper into the fast, I became acutely aware of my body's remarkable intelligence. It started sourcing nourishment from within, tapping into its reserves. This process, often misunderstood or ignored, is a testament to the profound adaptability of the human system.

After four days, the dry fasting phase came to an end, marked by a ceremonial water ritual. Sipping that first drop of water was like tasting life itself. The reintroduction of liquids, including water and diluted juices, was slow and deliberate over several days. The retreat facilitation team suggested a phased two-month protocol: a commitment to fluids only, with the option to reintroduce diluted soups or smoothies gradually after two weeks. This process felt like a dance between surrender and discovery, learning how to nourish the body in an entirely new way.

The purpose of this extended liquid phase went far beyond physical detox; it was about reconditioning the mind and body to shift away from the ingrained habit of chewing and, by extension, the deep-seated psychological ties we have to solid food.

Chewing is not just a mechanical process; it's something most of us do unconsciously throughout the day. It's tied to comfort, satisfaction, and even emotional regulation. The physical sensation of chewing has long been associated with feelings of fullness and satiety, making it one of the hardest habits to break. Over the years, we become conditioned to rely on this act as a signal of nourishment, even when we're not truly hungry. This protocol challenged that habit head-on, teaching the body to detach from the act of chewing and instead recognize that nourishment can come in other forms, such as through liquids, energy, and even through the breath.

For the first two weeks of the protocol, the commitment was strict: only liquids in the form of water and diluted juices, allowing the digestive system a prolonged period of rest. This step wasn't just about providing sustenance in a different form; it was about reawakening the body's natural intuition and signaling systems, which habitual eating patterns had long overridden. Without the act of chewing, the body began to listen more intently to its real needs.

By the third week, the protocol allowed for the gentle reintroduction of more substantial liquids if we chose, such as thin soups or diluted smoothies, and still with an emphasis on maintaining the liquid form. The idea was to avoid re-triggering the old habit of chewing too soon, allowing the body to immerse fully in this new form of nourishment. By sustaining this liquid-only state for two months, participants were not only detoxing physically but were also undergoing a mental and emotional reset—a shift in how we perceive nourishment and fullness.

During this phase, I noticed a heightened awareness in my body.
The challenge of breaking the chewing habit also brought about a realization - how much of our relationship with food is rooted in habit and conditioning rather than true hunger. This protocol, though

physically demanding at times, offered an opportunity to reprogram not just the body's digestive responses but also the emotional and mental patterns tied to consumption. It was a journey of rewiring at a cellular level, stripping away layers of unconscious eating behaviors and reconnecting with a more intuitive, pure form of sustenance.

The Gap Between Retreat and Reality

While the retreat itself was immersive and powerful, I quickly noticed a glaring gap in the support structure once it was over. Except for occasional connections with fellow participants and independent research, there was little formal guidance post-program. For many, this gap was too vast, and within days, many participants returned to eating solid food, abandoning the idea of alternative nourishment. It highlighted the urgent need for a more comprehensive educational framework, one that includes not only physical detoxification and medical supervision but also mental, emotional, and spiritual detox.

The Aftermath: Physical Adjustments and Energetic Shifts

The two weeks following the retreat were by far the most challenging. While many people feel a surge of energy, for me, my body felt fragile, as if enormous, unfamiliar frequencies were pouring into me, dismantling old systems and demanding a total recalibration. It was as though my internal landscape had been shaken and stirred, no longer resonating with its former state and in desperate need of realignment. I was light both in body and spirit but also unsteady, as if I were caught between two worlds. Waves of dizziness and low energy washed over me, leaving me destabilized and unsure of my footing. During this time, bio-resonance assessments became my lifeline, offering insights into my body's fluctuating state as I monitored its progress, tracking the shift with keen attention.

This experience reminded me of cymatics, the science that shows how sound and frequency impact matter. If you sprinkle sand or salt onto a metal plate and expose it to a specific frequency, the particles arrange themselves into beautiful, intricate patterns. But here's the crucial part: before the particles align with the new frequency, they go into chaos.

The shift in frequency initially throws the sand into disarray, scattering wildly across the plate. Only once the frequency stabilizes do the particles settle into a new, harmonious pattern.

In much the same way, my body was experiencing a frequency shift. The old structures, patterns, and energies that had once governed my system were being disrupted by the new frequency pouring into me. The chaos I was feeling in the form of dizziness, low energy, and disorientation wasn't a sign of failure or breakdown. Rather, it was the natural precursor to realignment. Just like in cymatics, where chaos precedes the formation of a more refined and evolved structure, I intuitively felt my body was in the midst of reorganizing itself at a cellular level. This period of instability was not a regression but a necessary phase before my body could evolve to its new state of being.

This is a universal truth in both nature and personal growth - chaos often comes before evolution. Whether in nature or within us, periods of disruption or breakdown often signal that something greater is about to emerge. The old must dissolve to make way for the new, and that process can feel disorienting, even painful. But once the energy settles, you can find yourself in a more expansive and evolved state than before.

Slowly, the balance began to return. My strength increased, and I eventually found my rhythm, incorporating one day of dry fasting per week into my new nourishment routine. This only came after a full two months—a gradual process that allowed my body to fully attune to the deeper transformations occurring on both physical and energetic levels. Just as the particles in cymatics settle into a new, intricate design when the frequency stabilizes, my body, too, found its new resonance, aligning with a higher state of nourishment and energy.

Now, one day of dry fasting each week has become a key part of my routine as a way to reset my system, both physically and energetically. This regular practice acts as a gentle reminder to the body, allowing it to recalibrate and maintain balance without the strain or discomfort I experienced during the retreat. Interestingly, the dry fasting I do now feels vastly different from that initial experience. Gone are the dry mouth and detox symptoms that once left me feeling drained. Instead, my body moves through the day with ease, tapping into its innate ability to regenerate. It's as though the discomfort was merely part of the body's adjustment period, and now that I've aligned with this new way of being, dry fasting has become a natural, almost effortless process.

This weekly practice of dry fasting, which once seemed like a challenging endeavor, has evolved into an integral part of my life, serving as a gateway to maintaining balance and vitality. With this transformation, I began to explore the broader principles of dry fasting and its powerful detoxification potential.

Dry Fasting: A Gateway to Deep Detoxification and Healing

The practice of dry fasting is not a modern health trend; it stretches back through the annals of history, intertwined with ancient cultures, myths, and spiritual practices. Over time, humanity has understood the power of fasting, not just for physical health but for spiritual awakening and deep purification.

Take, for example, the story of the Greek philosopher Pythagoras. Known for his mathematical genius, Pythagoras was also a mystic who believed deeply in the power of fasting. Before he would initiate new students into his secretive school of wisdom, Pythagoras required them to undergo extended periods of fasting—both from food and, at times, water. He believed that fasting heightened mental clarity enhanced spiritual insight, and brought the body into a state of purity. According to historical records, Pythagoras himself practiced dry fasting to prepare for major intellectual and spiritual breakthroughs, recognizing the connection between physical purification and the elevation of consciousness.

In ancient Egypt, the priests who served in the temples of Amun-Ra engaged in periods of dry fasting as part of their sacred rites. They believed that abstaining from food and water allowed them to commune more closely with the gods, entering altered states of consciousness where divine knowledge could be revealed. Fasting in these ancient times wasn't merely an act of physical cleansing; it was considered a powerful conduit for receiving wisdom from the universe.

Similarly, in Indigenous cultures, fasting has long been used as a method of spiritual vision and personal growth. The Native American practice of the *vision quest* involved young initiates going into the wilderness for days without food or water, seeking guidance from the spirits. It was believed that only by stripping away physical sustenance could one receive deeper spiritual nourishment and profound insight. Fasting was seen as a means of shedding the physical to transcend into higher states of being, and it is a philosophy echoed in many traditions.

Even in religious texts, you will find echoes of dry fasting's significance. These stories point to a recurring theme across civilizations: that fasting is not only a path to physical renewal but also a gateway to profound spiritual transformation.

Characterized by complete abstinence from both food and liquid intake, dry fasting is one of the most potent methods for detoxification and physiological renewal. Advocates often suggest that the benefits of a single day of dry fasting may be equivalent to three days of water fasting, underscoring its remarkable healing potential. But for many, this practice is shrouded in mystery and often misunderstood.

Personally and intuitively, I believe dry fasting holds the key to "flipping the switch" to Source feeding, bridging the gap between reliance on external nourishment and the body's inherent capacity to sustain itself. Over time, my own experiences, along with research, have reinforced this belief and dispelled the many myths surrounding dry fasting. It's not the dangerous, reckless endeavor that many believe it to be, but rather a powerful method of unlocking the body's natural ability to heal and regenerate. The fear that one cannot survive more than three days without water is rooted in outdated conditioning, not in the reality of the body's remarkable intelligence.

Does Eating Hinder Healing

Throughout history, cultures have observed that the body's natural response to illness is often a loss of appetite. This instinctual wisdom, when the body is unwell, is to shift focus from digestion toward healing. The question we should ask is not whether eating is necessary during illness, but rather, "Does eating hinder the healing process?"

Consider how, when you're sick, your desire for food diminishes. This is the body's way of redirecting its energy toward recovery. Yet, despite this natural signal, we are often encouraged—by well-meaning friends and family—to eat, even if our body is clearly telling us otherwise. Dry fasting taps into this wisdom, allowing the body to use its resources for deep healing, unburdened by the constant demands of digestion.

One of the most profound processes triggered by dry fasting is *autophagy*. This critical survival mechanism activates the body's ability to protect the brain and muscles while simultaneously cleaning cells, restoring metabolic function, and providing materials to rebuild new cells. The word "autophagy" comes from the Greek words *auto* (self) and *phagy* (to eat), literally meaning "self-eating." During this process, the body eliminates damaged, degenerate, or senescent cells (cells that no longer function properly but haven't died), like clearing out the clutter to make room for fresh, healthy growth.

It's like the metaphor of "one bad apple spoiling the bunch." If the body isn't allowed to clear out these dysfunctional cells, they can begin to affect the health of surrounding tissues. Dry fasting, particularly when lasting over 10 hours, activates chaperone-mediated autophagy (CMA), which acts like a demolition crew, breaking down old, weak cells and preparing the body for renewal.

You may not have realized it yet, but you have already experienced dry fasting. Sleep itself is a form of dry fasting. Each night, when you stop eating and drinking, the body enters a natural period of repair and detoxification. Autophagy is activated during sleep, giving the body time to heal. However, if you constantly eat throughout the day and several times every day, this deep system repair is never fully activated. Eating stops the healing process, turning off autophagy and leaving the body in a state of perpetual maintenance rather than renewal.

The Body's Secret Water Supply

One of the most surprising and often misunderstood aspects of dry fasting is the body's ability to create its own water—endogenous water. Conventional wisdom tells us that water is essential for life and that going without it is dangerous. However, this belief overlooks the body's ability to generate water internally. Russian doctors discovered that drinking external water actually stimulates gastric juices and disrupts the transition to endogenous nourishment. When we stop consuming water, microbes, viruses, and parasites that thrive in the water die off quickly, allowing the body to enter a deeper state of detox.

Where does this endogenous water come from? The answer lies in our fat cells. After about three days of dry fasting, the body depletes its glycogen stores and begins converting fat into energy and water. This process takes place within the mitochondria of our cells, meaning that each of the trillions of cells in the body is capable of producing its own water. During my own dry fasts, I've experienced this firsthand—my body, instead of feeling thirsty, begins to efficiently generate its own internal hydration, making the process of dry fasting far less taxing than many believe.

Endogenous water, produced by the body, is vastly different from exogenous or external water. When we drink external water, the body must restructure the water molecules and remove impurities, requiring energy and time. However, the water produced internally is already structured, pure, and aligned with the body's needs. This "living water" revitalizes the blood and lymph, helping to detoxify the body on a cellular level.

Moreover, dry fasting is one of the most effective ways to reduce harmful deuterium levels in the body—an important factor in the process of DNA repair, which plays a key role in longevity and overall health.

DNA Repair and Stem Cell Activation: The Fountain of Youth?

If your lifespan is compromised by DNA damage, then dry fasting offers a pathway to repair. Autophagy, as activated by dry fasting, can actually demethylate DNA, repairing cellular functions and potentially reversing the effects of aging. However, perhaps one of the most exciting benefits of dry fasting is its ability to awaken stem cells. After about three days of dry fasting, insulin production stops, signaling stem cells to enter regenerative mode. These stem cells are like the superheroes of our body, capable of transforming into different types of cells—muscle, blood, and even brain cells. Just like a bag of Lego bricks, they can be used to build many different things, and stem cells can change into different types of cells, such as muscle cells, blood cells, or brain cells. This ability makes them important for helping our bodies grow, heal, and repair themselves.

In fact, a study by researchers at MIT found that just 24 hours of fasting could reverse age-related loss of stem cell regeneration, particularly in the gut. Extending dry fasting to seven days can activate enough stem cells for whole-body restoration, offering a powerful tool for deep healing and regeneration.

Perhaps one of the most fitting metaphors for dry fasting is the ancient myth of the Phoenix, the legendary bird that, upon reaching the end of its life, builds a nest and sets itself aflame. Out of the ashes of its own destruction, the Phoenix is reborn, renewed, purified, and vibrant with new life. This cycle of death and rebirth symbolizes the process of dry fasting. As the body enters the "starvation" state, old, damaged cells—the ashes of our past—are burned away through autophagy. In their place, new, healthy cells emerge, leading to physical rejuvenation and renewal.

Just as the Phoenix must endure the fire to rise again in a higher, more refined form, the body, too, must go through a period of stress during a dry fast to activate its deepest healing potential. The old systems must be dismantled for something more vibrant and life-affirming to take root. This ancient myth beautifully mirrors the transformative power of dry fasting, showing that from chaos and destruction comes rebirth and regeneration.

Re-Imagine
YOU

If you're inspired to experiment with dry fasting, then let me offer you some tips and guidelines to ease into this experience to make it easy for you:

Start Gradually: Begin by implementing shorter periods of dry fasting. For instance, you might start with a 12-hour fast and gradually increase the duration as you become more comfortable.

Stop Drinking Liquid Earlier: Aim to stop consuming any liquids 2-3 hours before bedtime. This will help you start your dry fast with a natural 8-10-hour overnight fasting period.

Resist Nighttime Temptations: Avoid the urge to drink water during the night. If you wake up thirsty, remind yourself that it's part of the process and focus on resting.

Breathe Through Your Nose: To avoid your mouth becoming dry, try to breathe through your nose rather than your mouth. This simple adjustment can help maintain comfort during the fast.

Listen to Your Body: Pay attention to how you feel throughout the fast. If you experience extreme discomfort or dizziness, it's okay to break your fast and try again another day.

Prepare for the Fast: Ease into the fasting experience by consuming light, easily digestible foods before starting. This can help prevent discomfort and prepare your digestive system.

Rest and Relax: Take it easy during your dry fasting period. Engage in gentle activities like reading or meditating and avoid strenuous exercise, which can increase dehydration.

Rehydrate Properly After the Fast: When breaking your fast, start with small sips of water to rehydrate slowly. Follow with light, nutritious foods to help your body adjust back to regular eating… it's not about rushing back to burgers, pizza, and chips – respect your body.

And finally, please be sensible and use common sense. If you have health challenges, then you will need to fast or detox under medically supervised conditions. It's about healing your system and not harming it!

Think of your body as a garden. Just as a garden needs time to rest and rejuvenate to grow stronger, your body benefits from periods of dry fasting. It's like giving your garden a winter break, allowing the soil to restore its nutrients and prepare for new growth. Similarly, dry fasting offers your body and mind the chance to reset, heal, and emerge more vibrant and resilient.

You can approach dry fasting mindfully and effectively, helping you explore its benefits while ensuring a safe and positive experience.

"In the stillness of dry fasting, the body taps into its own profound wisdom, accessing the healing power of endogenous water. This inner reservoir cleanses, rejuvenates, and renews, guiding you back to your natural state of balance and vitality."

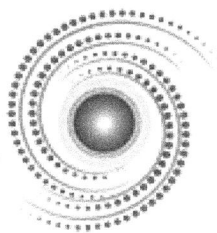

Chapter Eleven

Reimagining Your Potential
Through Source Feeding

KEY QUESTIONS:

How would your life change if you embraced nourishment
beyond physical sustenance?
What would it mean to be free from traditional needs for food,
energy, or sustenance?

This journey of bioregenesis - of activating the full potential of your DNA and moving toward Source feeding - is not a destination but a dance, an ongoing evolution. Just as the universe expands and shifts, so too do you, constantly reimagining your relationship with nourishment, energy, and consciousness. The path is not linear; it is filled with spirals of growth, moments of doubt, and breakthroughs that defy our previous understanding.

This is the dance of life, an ever-changing rhythm that invites you to shed the layers of conditioning you've acquired over lifetimes. As I continue on this path, I realize that Source feeding is more than just learning how to live without physical food—it's about rediscovering the boundless energy that resides within us and unlocking our true potential as multidimensional beings.

Nourishment From Within

In my own practice, the transition to Source feeding has been deeply intertwined with grounding techniques that connect me to the Earth's energy. Like a tree with deep roots, my connection to the Earth provides stability while allowing me to reach for higher frequencies. Sun gazing, for example, has become a powerful tool for absorbing solar energy, much like photosynthesis, nourishing my body and expanding my vitality.

Meditation plays a key role in this process, as it allows me to access higher states of consciousness, where I can align with the frequencies necessary for Source feeding. Through techniques like Quantum Morphogenetic Activation, Psonns, Codes, and Visualization, I am able to activate the energetic pathways within my physical atomic structure, unlocking deeper levels of bioregenesis. This isn't a static process—it's a continuous evolution, one where I experience profound shifts in consciousness often mirrored in my physical body's vitality.

The idea of living without food may sound radical to modern ears, but it is an ancient practice rooted in spiritual traditions around the world. In the stories of great sages and mystics, we find evidence of individuals who transcended the need for physical nourishment. The yogi Prahlad Jani, who lived without food or water for decades, claims he sustained himself entirely by a substance he described as Amrita, the nectar of immortality. In Hindu mythology, Amrita is the divine essence that grants eternal life, and its appearance in Jani's story is a reminder that the ability to be nourished by pure energy is not a new idea—it is an ancient truth long forgotten in our age of excess.

You will see similar themes not only in the Bible but across various spiritual traditions. In Islam, for example, the practice of fasting during the holy month of Ramadan is not only a physical discipline but a spiritual purification. Muslims fast from dawn until sunset, refraining from food and drink as a means of drawing closer to God. Physical abstention serves as a reminder of the soul's deeper connection to divine energy, and through fasting, believers aim to strengthen their faith and spiritual awareness.

These stories and practices are not just historical or religious customs; they serve as powerful metaphors for the deeper spiritual nourishment that sustains us when we align with higher frequencies.

Breaking Free From Conditioning

One of the greatest challenges on the path to Source feeding is breaking free from the conditioning that tells you that you must eat to survive. We are bombarded with messages that equate food with comfort, identity, and even love. But what if these messages are just part of the mass programming that keeps you disconnected from your true potential?

In my own journey, I have faced moments of doubt where the urge to return to old eating habits was strong. Each time, I reminded myself that this path is about more than just food—it's about freedom. It's about liberating myself from the need to rely on external sources for sustenance and realizing that the power to nourish myself comes from within.

One of the most common questions I'm asked is, "Don't you get hungry?" The truth is, I rarely feel hunger in the traditional sense anymore. And on the rare occasions when I am tempted by food, I pause, check within, and realize that I already feel full and nourished by a deeper source of energy. This brings up an even more important question: *What am I really hungry for?*

Hunger, for many people, is not always a physical need but an emotional or psychological one. Food often satisfies something deeper, perhaps a longing for comfort, a desire for distraction, or a way to fill a void that has nothing to do with physical sustenance. By embracing Source feeding, I've had to confront these underlying emotions and ask myself, *What is it that I really want to nourish?*

This awareness has allowed me to break free from the unconscious habits of reaching for food out of boredom, stress, or habit. Instead, I tune into my body's true needs and realize that, more often than not, it is already full, sustained by the life force energy I've learned to align with.

Navigating Social Situations

One of the most beautiful realizations on this path is that you do not have to isolate yourself or cut off from your friends and family. Social situations involving food can still be enjoyed. In fact, I have been fortunate to have a supportive circle of friends who understand my path, and my lifestyle doesn't require me to constantly be around people who are eating. When I do find myself in such situations, I don't feel pressured to eat. Instead, I may enjoy a cup of tea or diluted juice, engaging in the experience without the need to consume food.

This is an important distinction: Source feeding doesn't mean cutting off from the world or becoming a recluse. It's about learning how to be nourished in a new way while still participating in life's experiences. You don't have to isolate yourself or forgo social connections. In fact, it's about expanding those connections to include deeper conversations and experiences that aren't centered around food.

There's a wonderful metaphor in this: imagine being at a banquet, but rather than focusing on the food, you are there to savor the company, the conversation, and the shared energy of the people around you. You can enjoy the richness of life without needing to partake in the physical meal because true nourishment comes from connection, joy, and presence.

The Resistance to Source Feeding: Why Research is Scarce

Despite the profound potential of Source feeding, it remains on the fringes of mainstream scientific thought. In fact, Source feeding is still seen by many as the stuff of science fiction, with those who follow this path often ridiculed or accused of lying about their practices. Even when studies have been conducted, many have remained unpublished despite the promise to share the results, highlighting the reluctance within the scientific community to engage with this phenomenon openly.

One of the most striking examples is Prahlad Jani, who underwent stringent medical assessments to validate his claim of living without food and water for decades. While his case should have sparked serious scientific inquiry, it was largely dismissed, with many in the medical community refusing to believe the results. Even today, scientific findings like those of Dr Gerald Pollack, who explores the idea that the body can sustain itself on light, are often ignored or ridiculed, as they challenge the very foundations of what we believe about human nutrition.

A powerful documentary, *In the Beginning There Was Light* by P.A. Straubinger, explored these possibilities, yet the subject remains controversial. One Source feeding advocate shared with me that, while they had found scientists who supported the potential of this path, those scientists feared losing funding and credibility if they publicly endorsed it. The result is that Source feeding remains a step too far for a society that is conditioned to overeat, overdrink, and consume excessively.

Dean Radin, MS, PhD, Chief Scientist at the Institute of Noetic Sciences (IONS), offers a compelling explanation for why research on Source feeding is so scarce. In his view, the sheer magnitude of the claim—that humans can live without food—makes it too radical for the scientific community to take seriously. He states, "Perhaps the most curious aspect of the breatharian tests is the in-your-face nature of the claimed phenomenon, and yet an almost complete lack of interest from the scientific community. If it is possible to live well without eating food, this ought to be easy to demonstrate, and if it held up, the scientific and social consequences would be astounding. The fact is, as with many other observed phenomena that science cannot explain, most researchers regard things like this as ridiculous and extremely unlikely, and therefore do not even take the time to look into them."

This reluctance is rooted in the comfort of established paradigms. Acknowledging Source feeding as a reality would require a fundamental shift in how we understand human biology and nourishment—a shift that the scientific community, and indeed society as a whole, is not yet ready to embrace.

Source Feeding Isn't For Everyone: Where Do YOU Start?

It's important to recognize that Source feeding is not for everyone. After all, not everyone is at the right point in their life, and that's alright. For some, the journey to Source feeding is a gradual process of aligning with higher frequencies, and for others, it may not be the path they are called to follow in this lifetime.

So, where do YOU start? The first step is breaking free from the mass programming and conditioning around food. Begin by acknowledging your multidimensionality and understand that your body and DNA hold the potential for far more than you've been led to believe. Repairing your DNA is critical if you want to evolve and expand your consciousness.

Consider starting with practices like intermittent fasting or regular detoxing—not just physically but mentally, emotionally, and spiritually. Detox your mind by reducing your consumption of social media and toxic news. Detox emotionally by addressing the deeper feelings you've been masking with food. And detox spiritually, allowing yourself to release the beliefs and conditioning that have kept you tethered to old paradigms.

This is where you begin the journey to becoming the Avatar, Master, and Guru. By detoxing on every level—physically, mentally, emotionally, and spiritually—you start to peel back the layers that have been masking your true potential. You begin to *re-imagine* yourself in a more expansive, brilliant way.

By taking the first steps and by choosing to *re-imagine* who you are and how you live, you can unlock new levels of vitality, consciousness, and freedom.

Ethical Considerations: A Path of Responsibility

As you venture into the realms of Source feeding, it's essential to approach this path with transparency and responsibility. Source feeding, as a means of DNA regeneration and activating Higher Sensory Perception, offers transformative potential and requires careful consideration. This is not a path to be taken lightly, nor should it be promoted without acknowledging the potential risks alongside the profound benefits.

Every individual embarking on this journey must be empowered to make informed decisions. That begins with understanding both the risks and rewards of alternative dietary practices like Source feeding. It's crucial to approach this lifestyle with respect for one's own body and unique circumstances. Just as with any significant life change, the safety and well-being of individuals must be the highest priority, especially when experimenting with nutritional interventions that push the boundaries of conventional understanding.

For those participating in research or experiential programs related to Source feeding, comprehensive screening for pre-existing health conditions and careful monitoring throughout the process are non-negotiable. This ensures that the practice supports the individual's well-being rather than undermining it. Additionally, avoiding sensationalism and misinformation when sharing experiences with others is key. The practice of Source feeding should never be portrayed as a magical solution or quick fix but rather as a deeply personal journey of growth, evolution, and alignment with higher energies.

Finding Your Own Path

Source feeding is a deeply individual experience, and not everyone is meant to walk this path. It's about frequency and being a frequency match to the lifestyle and its energetic requirements. If you're not ready to make the leap, that's perfectly fine. Each person must decide for themselves what works best at their current stage of evolution. It's important to understand that this is not a one-size-fits-all journey. Some may resonate with Level 1, enjoying occasional Source feeding while still consuming food; others may embrace the more advanced levels.

Your journey to Source feeding also depends on your environment and lifestyle. If you're surrounded by an unsupportive family or working in a fast-paced environment that reinforces unhealthy habits, it may be more difficult to fully embrace this way of living. The key is to build a supportive network, one that nurtures your growth and aligns with your path.

You live in a world inundated with toxins from the food you eat, the water you drink, the air you breathe, even the products you use on your skin, the clothing you wear, and household products. These toxins burden your body, although often masked by promises of convenience or quick fixes. The reality is that many of the health challenges many people face, both physically and mentally, are rooted in the toxic load that is endured daily.

Thankfully, there is hope. Your body is inherently designed to maintain balance and vitality, given the right environment. Source feeding offers a way to step into alignment with your body's natural healing mechanisms, allowing you to detoxify and nourish yourself on a profound level. This path isn't just about removing physical toxins; it's about mental, emotional, and spiritual detoxification as well. By shedding the conditioning that has kept us attached to old patterns of eating, thinking, and being, we can rediscover our true potential.

Imagine a tree standing tall in a vast, open field. For years, it has relied on the soil and rain to grow, drawing nourishment from the earth and sky. But one day, the tree begins to realize that its strength, vitality, and growth are not solely dependent on external elements. It taps into a deeper source of nourishment—an inner wellspring of life force that flows from within. As the tree draws from this internal reservoir, it grows more vibrant, its leaves brighter, and its branches stronger. The external elements still play their part, but the tree no longer depends on them for survival. It thrives from within, connected to the very essence of life that permeates the universe.

This is the essence of Source feeding: a journey toward inner nourishment, where you are no longer reliant on external sources for sustenance but are fueled by the boundless energy of life itself. The process is deeply transformative, revealing the extraordinary capacity of the body for self-renewal and healing.

A Holistic Approach to Re-Imagining You

Embracing Source feeding invites you to reimagine what true nourishment looks like. It's not just about eliminating physical food; it's about aligning with the most fundamental energies of the universe. This path asks you to question deeply ingrained beliefs about what your body truly needs to thrive.

On this journey, you will witness your body's natural intelligence as it adapts to new ways of being, shedding attachments to food and emotional patterns tied to eating. For some, it is an easy and natural transition, and for others, it's not easy. After all, letting go of comfort, identity, and habits can be challenging. But in doing so, you open yourself up to greater emotional freedom and clarity. You'll discover that you no longer need food as an emotional crutch because you are fully connected to the life force that sustains all things.

Beyond the physical and emotional dimensions, Source feeding catalyzes spiritual alignment. You'll find yourself tapping into higher states of consciousness, understanding that you are an integral part of the energy that flows through the universe. This alignment is where the true potential of bioregenesis lies. Regenerating your DNA is not just a biological process but a holistic, multidimensional transformation.

The Liberation of Being Source Fed

As I progress in my journey, I have found that Source feeding offers liberation rather than deprivation. It is a path where nourishment no longer comes from the outside but from within. And with that comes the freedom to choose how you engage with physical food, if at all. Following this path does not mean rejecting food forever; it means having the power to decide whether or not you need it. Some days, I enjoy a taste of food or a sip of juice, not out of hunger, but simply for the pleasure of it, knowing that I am no longer bound by the need to consume.

The benefits are extraordinary and include enhanced vitality, heightened creativity, and an expanded sense of spiritual awareness. As the body cleanses and the mind clears, it's as though I am unlocking superhuman abilities that have been dormant all along. This is not magic. It is the natural result of aligning with higher frequencies and tapping into the full potential of the human body.

A Future of Infinite Possibilities

As you reach the end of this book, I invite you to reimagine yourself. What would it look like to live without the limitations that have defined your relationship with food, energy, and your own body? What if the key to unlocking your full potential lies not in what you consume but in what you *release*—the conditioning, the addictions, the limitations you've accepted for far too long?

The journey of bioregenesis and Source feeding is not just about changing how you eat; it's about reclaiming your birthright as a multidimensional being capable of far more than you've been led to believe. The path requires courage, dedication, and a willingness to question everything you've been taught. As I have experienced, the rewards are beyond measure.

In closing, I ask you to envision a future where you are not dependent on external sources for nourishment and are sustained by the limitless energy of the universe. Imagine a life where your body regenerates itself, where your DNA is constantly renewing, and where you are fully aligned with your highest self.

This is not a fantasy—it is a real possibility, one that countless individuals, including myself, have begun to explore. The key is to reimagine who you are and what you are capable of. You are not limited by your current understanding of nourishment or health. You are a being of energy and light, capable of aligning with the frequencies that sustain all life.

As you reimagine yourself, remember that this is an ongoing dance, a constant evolution of who you are becoming. The path to Source feeding is just one step in the greater journey of human potential, one that leads to a life of greater freedom, vitality, and connection to the universe.

This is about thriving and aligning yourself with the boundless energy that flows through all existence. It is an invitation to reclaim your innate power, reconnect with your true essence, and be more than you thought you could be

Embrace this journey with an open heart and a curious mind, knowing that the possibilities are infinite. You are capable of far more than you've ever imagined. It's time to *re-imagine you.*

Re-Imagine
YOU

You've reached the end of this book, but the journey to reimagine yourself is just beginning. This exercise is a sacred invitation to embody the wisdom you've discovered, align with your highest self, and step fully into your potential. Take the time to immerse yourself in the following steps. Let them guide you into the infinite possibilities that await.

1. Visualize Your Future Self

Close your eyes and imagine yourself five years from now, fully embodying the principles of Source feeding and multidimensional living.

- How does your body feel?
- How do you move through the world?
- What has changed in how you think, feel, and nourish yourself?

Write down 3-5 specific qualities or aspects of this future self.

2. Create Your Daily Practice

Choose one action or practice from the book that resonates most with you (e.g., sun gazing, meditation, grounding, fasting). Commit to integrating it into your life for the next 30 days.

- Track your experiences.
- Reflect on the shifts in your energy, mindset, and emotions.

3. Embrace the Question: "What Nourishes Me?"

Each time you feel drawn to food, drink, or distraction, pause and ask:

- "What am I truly hungry for?"
- "How can I nourish myself from within?"

Write these questions somewhere visible as a reminder to check in with yourself daily.

4. Visualize Your Infinite Self

Find a quiet space, free from distractions. Close your eyes and take a few deep breaths. Imagine a version of you that is free— free from conditioning, doubt, and limitation. Visualize yourself:

- Radiating boundless energy.
- Thriving without external dependencies.
- Fully aligned with the universe's rhythms and your soul's purpose.
  Feel this future self now. Ask:
- What would it feel like to wake up as this being each day?
- How would my choices and relationships shift?

Write down your answers as a roadmap to guide your evolution.

PART FIVE
SUMMARY

- Darkness strips away external stimuli, catalyzing a mental, emotional, physical, and spiritual detox, allowing you to detach from societal conditioning around food and discover inner sources of nourishment.

- Prolonged periods of darkness stimulate melatonin production, which aids in deep cellular repair, DNA regeneration, and heightened states of awareness. Darkness facilitates rest and rejuvenation, healing of cellular memory and the resolution of emotional imprints stored in DNA.

- The journey into darkness and Source feeding reveals the body's ability to create its own nourishment, including endogenous water, allowing for sustained vitality and detoxification without external food or drink.

- Dry fasting is a powerful method for detoxification, triggering autophagy—the body's process of clearing out damaged cells and regenerating healthy ones. It promotes deep cellular renewal and DNA repair and stimulates stem cell activation, promoting longevity and healing.

- During dry fasting, the body shifts from external hydration to producing its own structured, pure water from fat metabolism, highlighting the body's remarkable adaptability and intelligence.

- Dry fasting reduces harmful deuterium levels and eliminates parasites and microbes that rely on external water, allowing the body to reach a deeper state of detoxification and healing.

- Source feeding requires careful preparation, alignment, and an understanding that it may not be suitable for everyone. Success begins with detoxing physically, mentally, emotionally, and spiritually, paving the way for profound transformation.

- Source feeding offers a new paradigm of nourishment, where reliance on external food is replaced with connection to pranic energy. This shift fosters liberation, vitality, and alignment with your multidimensional nature.

The Dance of Becoming

Within you lies a spark unseen,
A light unbound, forever keen,
To free itself from earthly weight,
To rise, to flow, to resonate.

Beyond the hunger, past the need,
You find a path, a sacred creed,
Where nourishment transcends the form,
And feeds the spirit, pure and warm.

The stars they shine within your soul,
A universe, both vast and whole,
Aligned, attuned, no longer bound,
To limits once believed profound.

So, take this step, embrace the call,
For you are boundless, after all.
Reimagine, rise, become anew—
The endless dance of all you're due.

Dr. Carol Talbot

Afterword

An 'afterword' may be defined as someone other than the author who provides enriching comments or a section at the end of a book that describes the main text. In the case of Re-Imagine You, both definitions apply, and that being said, to provide enriching comments on a work so rich with revelation might be construed as excessive!

Dr. Carol has provided a roadmap and a virtual treasure map. The destination is nothing less than the creation or re-creation of what many would call 'hominum neo,' the human of the future. In the case of this book, Dr. Carol has the advantage of knowing that the 'man of the future' is also the man of our distant past. She is gifted with a purview of the true nature of space-time and deep knowledge of the history of our race that provides a larger framework, or context, in appreciating not only the content but the massive implications of what she has so diligently researched and organized in the book you now read. The scope of this book and its implications for individuals and as a race is nothing short of profound, given the critical juncture we and the planet find ourselves in. I believe that placing not only our experience of the world but also the quality of that experience front and center is the primary focus of this magnum opus. Re-imagine You deserve a very special position in a new category of books that specialize in self(less) help and that offer sincere and dedicated service to all.

One of the true riches of this book is that Dr. Carol has taken elements, most of which are taught in isolation, and combined them to create something that is far more powerful than looking at these elements in isolation. What is created by this is a phenomenon known as 'emergence,' whereby what is created by the interrelationship of various factors is truly more than simply the sum of its parts. In this way, this book is truly a holistic work. The sections of this book not only follow a logical sequence of both correlation and cause and effect, but they also weave a pattern of nested, interrelated concepts in which every section is not only an outgrowth building on the previous section but in which its essential character is retained across increasing ranges of scale, adding knowledge in fractal dimension.

Dr. Carol's experiences and revelations 'in the dark' are additional clues as to the genesis of Re-Imagine You. What the darkness implies is the 'void,' that place of stillness, where an all-permeating substance, known to the early Transcendentalists and New Thought authors as the 'unformed substance,' whose crystallization into form comes from our gift of thought, setting into motion the dynamic phase of mind, whereby the genesis of all forms begin to take shape. It's the 'prima materia' in the alchemical process, symbolized in many traditions such as the Black Madonna or Divine Creatrix.

In Re-Imagine You, Dr Carol has given us a glimpse of the future, our future as the 'Pure Human,' fed and nourished by the consciousness of Source itself. Finally, after a lifetime, or perhaps lifetimes of searching, through this book's unique perspective, we re-discover the true meaning of freedom and the revelation of ourselves as individuated expressions of the One True Source of All Things.

You have come to the end of a book but to the continuation of a journey whose destination is nothing less than the return to Oneness and Co-creatorship with the Divine. This is not a road less traveled; the path was clearly defined by those who have come before.

Now is the time to live it.
Philip Gruber

Appendix

Key highlights & Benefits of Source Feeding include:

1. **Potential for Bioregenesis**: Bioregenesis focuses on the body's inherent ability to repair and regenerate itself. It suggests that by using the body's natural regeneration capabilities, humans can heal and improve physical function, potentially reclaiming the original human DNA blueprint.

2. **Mass Programming and Consciousness**: The prevalence of mass programming contributes to collective ignorance and spiritual stagnation, impeding humanity's evolution towards higher consciousness.

3. **Energetic Dimension of DNA**: DNA functions as a transmitter of frequency, energy, and consciousness. It processes consciousness in a similar way to how film processes light in a projector, indicating that DNA is crucial in translating and transmitting frequency. Due to distortions in the template, as soon as consciousness comes into the physical atomic body and intertwines with the DNA template, the DNA template shuts off approximately 90% of the consciousness requirements. This means we do not remember our true cosmic history or remember ourselves as a multi-dimensional being.

4. **Activation of Dormant Potential for ESP**: According to Ashayana Deane, the dormant potential for extrasensory perception (ESP) exists within every individual. This potential can be activated through DNA functionality improvement, suggesting that removing distortions and blockages within the DNA structure could facilitate the reactivation of ESP. As distortions and blockages are gradually eliminated, the innate imprint for health is reawakened, and the genetic code expands its functionality by reassembling and activating currently dormant segments of the DNA blueprint. These changes facilitate a

gradual activation of higher sense faculties and an expansion of the human perceptual field to acknowledge our multi-dimensional anatomy. Tangible indicators of telepathic awakening include heightened perceptual acuity, more rapid manifestation of intentions, and awareness of the impact of thoughts on reality.

5. **Environmental and Dietary Toxins**: The presence of artificial additives, pesticides, and genetically modified organisms in our food supply and water has been shown to induce mutations and damage to our DNA, impairing cellular processes and hindering our evolution towards higher states of consciousness. These detrimental effects can also be passed down to future generations.

6. **Acknowledging the Frequency of Food**: The type of nutrition taken in makes a difference in the energy that can be converted and how efficiently our bodies can use that energy. Food and drinks laden with additives and potential carcinogens can impair cellular functions and the body's ability to efficiently convert food into energy. Each substance carries its unique energetic signature, influenced by factors such as its origin, preparation, and even the intentions imbued upon it. These frequencies, when ingested, interact with our own bioenergetic field, influencing not only our physical health but also our emotional and spiritual well-being. Thus, recognizing the energetic dimension of food, water, and drinks invites us to approach nourishment as a means of harmonizing and enhancing our overall energetic balance.

7. **Influence of Language and Thoughts on DNA**: Scientific studies have increasingly underscored the profound impact of language and thoughts on DNA expression and cellular function; therefore, the mental aspect, thought patterns, conditioning, and mass programming of an individual must be

considered in switching to Source feeding. Mental detox is an important key to success.

8. **Liberation from Hunger and Thirst**: Source feeding proposes the potential to transcend the biological need for conventional food and water, suggesting that humans can derive sustenance from prana, or life force energy, as demonstrated by the body's ability to absorb energy from the sun and transform it into vitamin D. If the ability is already available to transform the energy from the sun into vitamin D, it suggests the possibility of gaining other forms of nourishment from prana.

9. **Minimizing Exposure to Pollutants**: By reducing reliance on conventional sources of nourishment, individuals can harness the transformative potential of internal energy sources, which hold the promise for rejuvenating DNA and opening avenues for heightened states of consciousness and holistic well-being.

10. **Role of Sound in DNA Transformation**: Innovative research indicates that human DNA can be altered and reprogrammed using sound, with spoken words and phrases at specific frequencies successfully transforming cellular genomes. Because human DNA functions within a specific pattern of frequency, our sensory perception is intricately tied to the limited spectrum of frequencies perceived.

11. **Environmental Influence on DNA**: Environmental psychology suggests that our surroundings can reactivate youthful information in our cells, influencing our biological and genetic destiny.

12. **Source Feeding as a Holistic Approach**: Transitioning to Source feeding could minimize exposure to environmental toxins, rejuvenate DNA, and enhance overall well-being by providing sustenance through prana. By minimizing exposure to environmental toxins associated with conventional eating and drinking habits, breatharians seek to mitigate the risk of DNA damage and associated health issues. This practice and

lifestyle, through the research on dry fasting, has been found to create an environment where viruses, diseases, and parasites cannot exist. It also encourages the release of senescent cells and allows for the release of endogenous water as well as stem cells for repair. This controversial approach suggests that humans can thrive on minimal or no physical food intake, benefiting physically, emotionally, mentally, and spiritually.

13. **Benefits of Source Feeding**: Breatharians claim numerous benefits physically, emotionally, mentally, and spiritually, including enhanced vitality, mental clarity, less requirement for sleep, enhanced creativity, and accelerated spiritual growth.

14. **Freedom to Choose**: Source feeding is not about being deprived of anything but rather detaching from the addictive patterns of eating. It is different from fasting, which is not sustainable for long periods of time as there is still a dependence on physical nourishment. Being a Source fed means feeding and nourishment through a different source. It is having the freedom to choose to continue to drink water or diluted juice and have small tastes of food from time to time. This is not out of hunger but just for a change of taste, and there are different levels of being Source Fed to choose and experiment with.

15. **Successfully transitioning to Source Feeding**: There is no 8-day, 10-day, or 21-day program that is going to magically transform an individual to being successfully Source fed. Having personally attended two retreats, while all the attendees appeared to have benefited in some way from the experience, the majority returned to being nourished by physical solid food and liquid. It was either not the right time to make this transition, or they were seeking a detox experience, or in the case of the Darkroom, a spiritual experience.

16. **Frequency Match**: According to Jasmuheen, it is crucial to have a frequency match or be close to the frequency of source

feeding to transition easily and without detrimental effects on the physical body. The survey results cited in Jasmuheens' book, Ambassadors of Light, highlight the importance of those interested in this path already having a lifestyle that includes a strong and regular spiritual practice, and a certain level of belief, awareness, and lifestyle.

17. **Recommendation for a Comprehensive Approach to Source Feeding**: Successfully transitioning to a pranic lifestyle requires a comprehensive program that addresses physical, mental, emotional, and spiritual detoxification. Education is required first to awaken people to the mass conditioning and programming that encourages our addiction to food and drink and challenge the mainstream narrative and misinformation that is prevalent about our actual nutritional requirements from food and drink. Any program should include a sustained practice incorporating teachings and techniques to harness energy, a strong support element, and medical markers, all of which are essential for transitioning to and maintaining this lifestyle.

Re-Imagine YOU, Bioregenesis of the Human DNA Blueprint through Source Feeding offers a transformative potential for human evolution, emphasizing the profound interconnectedness between our bodies, environment, and higher states of consciousness.

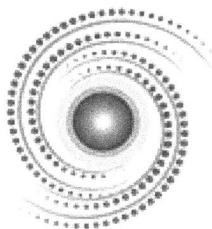

References & Resources

Chapter One
Baird T. Spalding – *The Life & Teachings of the Masters of the Far East*
Max Freedom Long – *The Secret Science Behind Miracles*
Charles Haanel – *The Master Key*
Kosta Danaos - *The Magus of Java*
Ashayana Deane – *Voyagers I & II*

Chapter Two
Daniel Estulin PhD - *Tavistock Institute*
Preston Nichols – *The Music of Time*

Chapter Three
Blake Crouch – *Dark Matter*

Chapter Four
William Bramley – *The Gods of Eden*
Dr Glen Rein – *study titled Consciousness and the New Biology of DNA*
David A. Sinclair PhD – *Lifespan: Why we Age – and Why We Don't Have To*

Chapter Five
Candace B. Pert – *Molecules of Emotion*

Chapter Six
Dr Edward Bach - *The Twelve Healers and Other Remedies*
Deuterium Depleted Water – *www.drinklitewater.com*

Chapter Seven
Hilton Hotema – *Man's Higher Consciousness*
P.A. Straubinger – *In The Beginning was Light – documentary*
Dr Gerald H Pollack – *The Fourth Phase of Water*

Chapter Eight
Jasmuheen – *Ambassadors of Light*
Michael Werner – *Life from Light*

Chapter Nine
Mantak Chia – *www.mantakchia.com*
Carlos Castaneda – *Journeys to Ixtlan*

Chapter Ten
August Dunning – *The Phoenix Protocol*
Sergey Filonov – *20 Questions & Answers about Dry Fasting*

Chapter Eleven
Bioregenesis Academy – *https://www.bioregenesisacademy.org/*
Breatharian World – *www.breatharianworld.com*
Jasmuheen – *www.jasmuheen.com*
The Possibility Hub – *www.thepossibilityhub.com*

About the Author

Dr. Carol Talbot's voice is a spark of transformation—when she speaks, people listen, laugh, learn, and sometimes even walk across burning coals. A master of transformation, a catalyst for change, and a guide for those ready to awaken their highest potential, Dr. Carol is the Founder and Creator of The Possibility Hub and a passionate ambassador for expanding consciousness and unlocking the superhuman abilities inherent within us all. Her mission is to take individuals beyond their perceived boundaries, opening them to a world of new possibilities and expanded awareness.

With a PhD in Quantum Morphogenetic Science, Dr. Carol's pioneering research on DNA bioregenesis and Source Feeding is reshaping our understanding of human potential. Her journey has led her to study with extraordinary masters and participate in transformative experiences. Dr. Carol believes that to truly reimagine ourselves, we must detox on every level—mentally, emotionally, physically, and spiritually—to cleanse the layers of conditioning and embrace the truth of our multi-dimensional nature.

Her wisdom and insights are drawn from exploring both ancient traditions and cutting-edge science. Known for her ability to distill complex ideas into practical, life-changing wisdom, Dr. Carol helps people shift their perspectives to see the greater game in which we all play. She teaches that by embracing our true multidimensionality, we can unlock hidden potential, heal at deeper levels, and step into a more expansive version of ourselves. Her approach goes beyond self-help; it is about reimagining the very fabric of who we are, at the deepest levels.

Dr. Carol's programs, retreats, and experiences are designed to offer more than personal growth—they encompass a multi-dimensional perspective, allowing individuals to tap into the full spectrum of their existence. As an NLP Master Trainer and Certified Master Firewalk Instructor, she uses a diverse range of tools, from Quantum Morphogenetic Physics to Time-Line Therapy™ ,Sound Healing and Bio-Geometry, to ignite rapid transformation and help others master their reality.

Through her podcasts, retreats, and mentoring programs, Carol invites you to evolve, expand, and experience a profound connection to the limitless potential within and a more expansive understanding of who you truly are.

Dr. Carol Talbot invites you to detox, reimagine, and embrace your multidimensional self—because the real magic begins when you re-imagine YOU.

www.caroltalbot.me   www.thepossibilityhub.com

www.ingramcontent.com/pod-product-compliance
Lightning Source LLC
Chambersburg PA
CBHW030929090426
42737CB00007B/366